Rite of Lilith

by John F. Rychlicki III

"I am the snake that devoured the spirit of man with the lust of light. I am the sightless storm in the night that wraps the world about with desolation. Chaos is my name, and thick darkness. Know thou that the darkness of the earth is ruddy, and the darkness of the air is grey, but the darkness of the soul is utter blackness."

- LIBER XXX AERUM vel Saeculi sub figvra CCCCXVIII
The Vision and the Voice, Call of the 14th Aethyr

Crucible Publications LLC

Rite of Lilith
Copyright © 2017 John F. Rychlicki
III All rights reserved.

To order wholesale, please contact:
American Wholesale Book Company (205) 956-4151
Ingram Book Company (800) 937-8000
Baker & Taylor (800) 775-1100

Crucible Publications Phoenix Arizona, 85008 U.S.A.

Crucible Publications is a publishing house for the 21st century, not the 20th.

Crucible Publications produces & invests in neoteric and visionary artists, writers, and musicians bringing an unconventional vision of art and literature. The company began in 2008 to produce the works of renaissance and neoteric oriented creators, leading us into the 21st century.

TABLE OF CONTENTS

Preface 4

I Semitic Occultism 6

II Call of the Nosferatu 13

III Rite of Lilith 22

IV Apocrypha of Lilith 36

V The Black Madonnas 46

VI Ad cubavit lamia 57

VII The Black Kabbalah 63

VIII The Origins of Lilith 95

IX The Grottos of Lilith 100

X Lailah and Naamah 129

XI Rite of Naamah 134

Bibliography 142

Preface

Now and again, you hear near whispers, coiling, snaking around Man and his gods. Sibilant, serpentine whispers that beckon you to the edge of sanity, ever-wailing, ever-screeching. Silently peering across the endless desert, sits *Lilith*...the dreaded black goddess. Hidden behind walls of Temples, Lodges, Mosques, Churches, are vessels of the cursed, the pungent perfumes of rotted children and the aroma of Judaic sacrifices. And in racial memories of the dead with their necromantic bacchanalia, *Lilith* hisses endlessly in her grottoes, hidden in the Space between the spaces. Your nightmares mesh with the remains of racial memories and incense smoke, cascading down to a crucible of endless pain.

All men have dreamt of Lilith...a shadow sashaying into your fantasies and mania. Lilith comes between you and the Sun, shutting out the vision of your gods. I have heard *Her*. You have heard *Her*. Hissing from deep within nightmares, luring you to the edge of the Void. She is the night without the Sun, whispers of her ghosts flicker in the ether, and in the living shadow, Her hissing reigns supreme. She is not the moon for her racial curse of the ancients and their Semitic progenies resides in your nightmares cascading down into a chrysalis of fading racial memory.

Lilith's symbolic cocoon of initiation lies in the habitations of the Kabbalistic Klippoth, the fallen and discarded Shells of Shells of creation. This deity, this unrelenting power, has been injected by the Semitic race into the depths of blood memory. She is anti-life, anti-culture, and the antithesis of mankind, love, and the human condition. Lilith's sign is the reddish star hanging lowly in the evening sky just beyond the desert, no astronomers dare name it, yet it portends the last days. It is the star used above the crescent moon on the banners and emblematic representations of Islam. The occult lunar initiations and magic are hidden deep within both Judaic and Islamic symbolism. The Islamic anthropomorphic attraction to the Kabah, pretending it is the devil, is the black Saturnic Cube of Death found in various ancient religions – all of which worship Lilith: the Black Goddess of Death.

I

Semitic Occultism

Lilith scholars Amy Scerba, M.A., and Dr. Barbara Black Koltuv trace the mythological motif of Lilith through Sumerian, Hebrew, Assyrian, Babylonian, Akkadian, Canaanite, and Persian cultural memes. Dr. Siegmund Hurwitz's precious 1992 exegesis, entitled *Lilith: the first Eve* (Hurwitz © 1992 Daimon-Verlag) approaches the Lilith motif as a psychological-religious case study. Dr. Hurwitz examines Lilith legends and more importantly her cultural etymology from both a historical and psychological standpoint.

The mythological motif of Lilith is a psychological- religious narrative that repeats across cultures. The multivalence of Lilith in ancient mythology compounds with syncretism in religious thought and fractures the borders between linear time and sacred place. Lilith's motif must not be used in a pejorative or dismissive study; the Judaic Talmudic curse of Lilith repeats itself infinitely against Abrahamic religious.

It is suitable for this series of studies to prospect the Lilith motif as a sexual-cultural prototype, as both an expression of the deepest regions of the Hebrew psyche, and an exhortation of the Judaic curse. The meta-narratives of Lilith breach barriers of psychological or religious memes hold preeminent effect on Jewish genotypes. Demythologizing Lilith does not sterilize the innate spirit of Her motif, it devalues the importance of Her various legends with hermeneutics.

Lilith and her iconography of fear and death present syncretic undertones of Judaic Kabbalist magic. According to the Talmud, the terrestrial world of matter must be judged on the conditions of the divine. Lilith therefore is not only a cursed deity repeating her motif across cultures, but a psychic and psychological anomaly in the blood of the 12 tribes of the Hebrews.

From the Serapic oracles of Isis, the wild Hunts of Artemis~Diana, the chthonic lore of Hecate and Demeter, ritual coitus dedicated to Inanna, among the cremation grounds of Hindu Kālī, Sumerian hymns to Ishtar, novenas to Mary Magdalene, and sado-masochistic sacrifices to Lilith, the black Goddess finds herself in every religious mythos. *She* is Not. Lilith is the psychic negation of the divine, and human love. Lilith's motif is the racial pain and spiritual darkness that inculpates mankind of the Fall from the divine hierarchy.

The black goddess of the Jews, has her ransom against mankind in the Talmud, and Zohar. The graveness of those who use black magic and Kabbalistic occultism lies in the failure to reconcile mankind's psychic and racial memory embedded in the blood and genome. Lilith's magic introduces the greatest possible separation from the divine origin; appealing to our resentments, vengeances, hatreds, sexual paraphilia; manifesting these as a Golem.

In the witch covens and guilds of ceremonial magic, "Lilith" is the *Scarlet Woman*. Sexual love embodied by the Scarlet Woman is the most carnal form of our obscure search to annex the psychic lines between Lust and Love. Aleister Crowley's Liber AL vel Legis reveals the Scarlet Woman as simply an anomaly to dispel Victorian Era sexual monstrosity: the lecherous Scarlet Woman whom is the consort of the Beast Mage is the source of all magic in Her *"is all power given."*
{Liber AL vel Legis}. John Whiteside Parson's "Babalon Working," speaks of the Scarlet Woman and Her concubine: *"For I am Babalon, and she my daughter, unique, and there shall be no other women like her. In My Name shall she have all power, and all men and excellent things, and kings and captains and the secret ones at her command."* {Liber XLIX; v.37-38}.

Magi invoke Lilith as the idealized woman failing to realize that therein Lilith's curse lies the origins of enmity between the Judaic tribes and mankind. Imposing their corrupt history and disobedience to God's Covenants, they cut off mankind from its tellar, divine, and extraterrestrial origins. Lilith's archetypal curse and repeating psychic imprint shortchanges the human condition into thousands of years of shadowed historic collusion; lightyears even away from scientific advancement into the spaces between the stars. Lilith's magic is initiatic treason against culture itself; against metaphysical blood and racial memory. Under Lilith's racial curse, sex has become warden, inquisitor, and judge of an entire race.

The Abrahamic religions is both anemic and manic from using sex as anesthesia. In the racialist Judaic covenants and doctrine, Lilith enables their historical pact of blood, one of the highest and most dangerous forms of black magic. Within the diablerie of occult Lodges who worship Lilith and the deity's resurging popularity manifesting feminist ideology, her worshippers become generic victims. The Kabbalists and their occultic enablers project racialist black magic and cultural failures onto themselves, and those outside their "chosen" race.

The archetypes of Lilith are debased. It is always Lilith, an evil demi-goddess who mingles black magick with racial mythology, and sex with diablerie. By cunning and deceit, Lilith's magick has won wars, enslaved entire city-states, and deprived Europe of her direction in the exodus of the left- turning Kali Yuga swastika; away from the enlightenment of the Mystery Schools, the fine arts, philosophy, and science.

Her black magick and its practitioners do not always declare themselves; many hide in contemporary paganism, witchcraft, political and social movements seeking to destroy the blood memory of mankind and its future descendants.

It is the racialist magick and archetypal repeating of Lilith that has wrought the conflict of gods and demons, of blood and races that finds no way out of Semitic curses. In context of ritual saturnalia, the hierodule {Greek, *hierodulous*}, served as a female sexual acolyte, often in connotation with ritualized prostitution. The religious prostitute referred to as the Scarlet Woman, allegorized as the Whore of Babylon in Revelations, was the sex-acolyte of bridal rites of Sumer, Canaan, ancient Persia and Mesopotamia.

The Rosi-Crucis was the sacred hieroglyph of the sex- acolyte, composed of a cross within a circle. The sigil is found in many ancient religious sites and Roman coinage. The ceremonial robes of the *heirodulai*, acolyte-prostitutes, were *scarlet red* because initiated courtesans engaged neophytes in ritual inverted coitus. The Jewish Song of Inanna reciprocated by the New Testament Song of Solomon presents part of an antiquated sex ritual.

Lilith is not the solace of sexual empowerment, she is manifestation of the Kali-Yuga, lunar-cursing, dragging the uninitiated into ruinous worlds that are shells of Shells. The racialist blood curse of LYLYT sees no way out in the struggle between gods and demons, Light and Darkness, there is no balance here. Erotic cults repeat Lilith's curse in the blood memory, lingering in novenas to Mary Magdalene, the cremation grounds of the Tantric Vāma-Kālī, the Carpocratians, and abbeys of the Black Madonna. Lilith and Her countless epithets in these cults is damned in print and song.

The *black goddess* is celebrated in erotic refrain after refrain in a parade of waiflike model-corpses across nightly entertainment, behind the veils of Muslimahs wailing in blood-filled mosques that infest ancient Babylon, She is the face of every frail beauty-Diva prostituted by corporate daddies, in the heroin needles of those whose only prayer is death, in the consensual rape of teenagers posing upon their digital and downloadable altars of self-adoration, Lilith is the face in the bulimic puke of would-be-doll-girls, behind a masochistic society where sex is at once a mania and anesthesia. Over and over, Lilith's sibilant refrain is heard in the blood memories of the crumbling bell-tower that is Western Civilization beset with the black goddess' racialist curse.

In the philosophy of the Hebrew Kabbalah, Lilith corresponds to the daemon of *Malchut* in the Qlifot {the World of Shells, or husks). Pertaining to Kabbalah every world is a husk of the world above and below. The Qlifot are shells of the dead worlds, explored by the lunar-initiates in opposition to the solar, the virile magic defined by Julius Evola. The result of any black magic, or adorations to Lilith is the death of the mind, and the spirit that binds mind and flesh together; Lilith throws these things into the vortex of the Kali-Yuga, the Dark Age of Earth under Abrahamic racialist black magick.

The racialist black magic and archetypal mania that

perpetuates its anti-nature ideologies and philosophies are leading mankind into the final slope of the Kali-Yuga. The powers that direct the drama of Semitic occultism are those of inertia, atrophy, and nothingness. That is to say, diablerie. The agents of disintegration have their way in the Current Year. Any workings towards LYLYT are of a one real force of spiritual destruction and imbalance in this half dead world.

"When society reaches a stage where property confers rank, where wealth becomes the only source of virtue, passion the sole bond between man, and wife, falsehood the source of success in life, sex the only means of enjoyment, and when outer trappings are confused with inner religion
. . . then we are in the Kali Yuga—the Dark Age."
—Vishnu Purana

The black magical power of the Semitic racialists, and Lilith worshippers is in direct opposition to the "Right-Hand Path," the "white magic" of the Western/Aryan Mystery Schools and their battlefield is the rest of the world which, is now a gray magical circle with a black center at Mount Sinai.

Etymological origins of Lilith independent of Jehovian-Semitic templates point to the Sumero-Babylonian *Lilû*, which translates to '*a demon equivalent to a male vampire.*' Derived from Sumerian, Lila refers to 'wind,' or 'storm.' Opting for Akkadian translations, scholars suggest *Lalu*, also Lulu as 'lecherous,' and 'wandering.'

From the Akkadian Lilitû and her Sumero-Babylonian compliments, Ardat-Lili, Idlu-Lili, and Lamaṣtû, derives the Semitic LYLYT {Lilith}. The Lilitû primarily feasted upon women and children, referred to by the terrified inhabitants of Ur and Babylon as night-ghosts that roamed the deserts away from populace. Pictographs from $800^{B.C.}$ to $500^{B.C.}$ Babylonia depict "Lilith" in the company of snakes and other abominable animals, keeping with themes of her malevolence in Babylonian pottery, Persian, and Jewish amulets and in the Qumran scrolls.

The night-ghosts here evolved into the Jehovian mythopoeia seeping into the Christian paradigms of diabolatry. Isaiah 34; xiv in the Vulgate refers to "he- goats," "hairy beasts," again carried over from Judaic paradigm. The Vulgate thusly reads; *"Et occurrent daemonia onocentauris, et pilosus clamabit alter ad alterum; ibi cubauit lamia, et inuenit sibi requiem."* Isaiah 34; xiv-xv refers to Lilith as the 'Screech Owl.'

The Apocryphal Gospel of Phillip states, *"If anyone becomes a child of the Bridal Chamber, he will receive the light. If anyone does not receive it while he is in these places, he will not be able to receive it in the other place. He who will receive the light cannot be seen, nor can he be held. And none can torment him while he dwells in the world. And furthermore, when he goes out of the world, already he has received the truth in images. The word has become the æon, for the æon has become for him the fullness. It is thus; it is revealed only to him. It is not hidden in the darkness and the night, but it is hidden in a perfect day and a holy light."*
{Gospel of Phillip 127}. Pascal Beverly Randolph, founder of the Fraternitatis Roseae Crucis stated to his initiates, *"sex is the Universe's most powerful force."* The **Rite of Lilith** uses this force to obtain unnatural psychic and spiritual abilities, and to plunge to lost soul further into a never-ending Night.

The accursed racialist black magicians of the Semitic race worship Lilith through the wilderness and desert isolation, in Her crucible of pain and the burial tombs of those dead but dreaming. Lilith's adorers and worshippers, be they in ritual witchcraft, politics, or philosophy, dwell in the unnatural path of fetish, within a failed genetic blueprint, captivating the darkest human fantasies. LYLYT dares you to walk alone...ever alone into the moonlit nightside crossroads where the journey begins between nightmare and flesh. LYLYT is the ruin of the human mind, the unbalanced manias, archetypes, and political movements "empowering women" through the Judaic sexual curse.

The **Rite of Lilith** unlocks pagan animism or polytheism, is to invert the previous religion's deities into antinomian "demons" as that side of their psyche becomes obscured. While **Lilitu** has its etymological origins in ancient languages of the Arab world, the name *Laylá* comes from the word *layl* meaning "night." Recall that Lilitu is associated with a night- ghost who roamed desolate places such as the

desert. Night represents the Unmanifest. In the Arabian deserts, the night is a reality without boundaries: forms are dissolved, no sand dunes or camels or anything else visible, all is formless, nothing but darkness. Spiritual blackness absorbs all light.
The Rite of Lilith unlocks the psyche hidden in the blackest depths of the mind.

The **Rite of Lilith** opens nightmares...fetishes....desires throughout the World's political movements, and underground secret societies tales of times remote; tales, who carry the remnants of books long turned to dust, tales, which whisper cryptically of Semitic devils. There are, born in each generation, Men and Women whom awake to memories and knowledge Lilith whispers in nightmares. The sibilant whispers of Lilith's magic revealed in this book for lost souls who speak the language of insanity and sanity.

There is no god in this Void. The serpentine whispers all conclude to one soft refrain. *Lilith.* A cult of devotees worships Her masks in dozens of cultures; they may or may not even know the allegiance they profess. They shall never have that which they desire, for there is *no revoking what has been called.* Let those last few words be a final warning to any lost soul attempting these rituals.

II

Call of the Nosferatu

Time
The Rite of Nosferatu is performed only on the night of the New Moon, during the sunset.

Acquirements
chalice, Scourge flail or instrument to draw blood, Frankincense, Myrrh, and Opium incense, fresh grave soil, spider {or worm}, 1 Red Candle Altar in West quadrant. A living spider is contained upon the altar.

Light a red candle. Sprinkle fresh grave soil around thee, circumambulate 3x counter-clockwise tracing the Ourobouros around your body; give Sign of the Cross with your hand upon each passing of the West. Thou shalt not fear the ghouls residing in the darkest wells of the mind, be firm in incantations, provident, and dutiful.

Return to the center of the chamber completing circumambulation of the Sun.

Recite:
Rise up and remember Nosferatu Recall the Promise once stain'd in blood on the Cross at Gol'goatha. Dying you are forgotten of death, rising you are poisoned by the deeds of Kaayin the Murderer. Nosferatu remember and receive the Body of Christ {give Sign of Cross}. Nosferatu remember and receive the Body of Christ {give Sign of Cross}. The Body of Flesh is cleansed and anointed. Go forth in mine own Chosen Body, the Temple of Yeheshvah Redeemer. Crown'd am I with thorns about the Horns of Judah. There is no part of me that is not I. My Hair is of the thorns that crucify, scourge and bless: the Sheaves of the Harvest and the Serpents of Fear; the Blood of the Shepherds, of Flower and Leaf; the Crown of the Lamb, the Threads that join the Stars, fair as the hair of the Queen of Sheba and fine as the Spider's web. My Face is the Sun and the Waning of the Moon, the Magdalene's tears and the Black Mirror of the Depths: Masks beyond Number concealing the Face of Nosferat! My Skull is the Conclave of

the White Eagle; mine is the Blessing, mine is the Curse. For I am the Voice of the Oracle Nosferat. My Eyes are the Twin Shewstones of Twilight, the Dawn and the Dusk. Bright as the Star of Morning, bright as the Star of Evening. Unto Nosferat is the Offering: the sacrifice of Virginity the abeyance of chastity. the Rhythms of Lust and the Words of the Black Madonna, the Voice of the Old Nosferatu, the Oracle of the Nosferatu. My Nose is the Guide of the Great Hunt, Keen as that of the Stag and the hound.

Unto Nosferat is the Offering: all Scents that madden and rouse the heart. My Mouth is the Sacrifice of the Red Serpent's Tongue, a bloodfeasting of Souls and a Receiving Grail. may I partake of the forbidden fruits sacrificed unto U-li-tu and Hivvah, incestuous Lilith and Eve. My Hands are the Shrines of Gol'goatha. My Skin is the Vestment of Sodom and Gomorrah. My Blood is the Ink of the Book of Nosferatu. My Shadow is the Twin. Serpent and Nosferat am I, conjoined in their Shadows the Twin Serpent Image of the Methuselah and antediluvian Nosferat. Nosophoros.

Necurat. Nesuferit. from the great blackness came I forth ere the blackness of Nod

i   - describe a circle about the crown of the head {thumb between index & medius}

ii   - thumb between index & medius {as before}, describe cross in the form of an 'X' upon the brow

iii   - as before, describe cross in the form of an 'X' upon the left temple

iv   - as before, describe cross in the form of an 'X' upon the right temple

v   - as before, describe cross in the form of an 'X' upon the left breast

vi   - as before, describe cross in the form of an 'X' upon the right breast

vii   - as before, describe cross in the form of an 'X' upon the genital I

Invocation of the Nosferatu

Face West; genuflect the dying Light {Sunset} and recite:

Draw near to me, come descend.. Draw near to me, come descend.. Draw near to me, come descend..
âhhazu..nosufuratu..vapir..vepir..upyr..
upier..pijauica..vlkodlak.. êdimmu..utukku
Hear me O Unclean, Fathers of Fatherhood, boundless shadow: iao iouo iao aoi oia psinother theropsin opsither nephthomaoth nephiomaoth marachachtha marmarachtha ieana menaman amanei israi amen amen
soubaibai appaap amen amen deraarai kakodaimonos kakodaimonos sasarsartou amen amen koukiamin miai amen amen iai iai touap amen amen amen main aio oai oai iao amen amen amen. I invoke you, plague-carriers, ye liars-in-wait, receivers of sin, receive the sins of souls of the unclean and infected, make me worthy to be reckoned in the Kingdom of Cain, Father of the Treasury of Sins, now I am unclean.
Father of Fathers, let the plague-bearers come who names are: Enchthonin, Charachar, Archaroch, Achrochar, Marchur, Lamchamor, Luchrir, Laraoch, Archeoch, Xarmaroch, Rochar, Chremaor. Hear me invoking you O Father of Fathers, receive the unclean ones.

Formulate the Klippotic Cross:
Touch brow and recite *Ateh She'ol* {thou art hell}
Touch breast and recite *Ge'hinnom* {and the depths of the earth}
Touch left shoulder and recite *ve-Tzelmoth* {the shadow of death}
Touch right shoulder and recite *ve-Shaari Moth* {the gates of death}
Touch genitals and recite *Edom* {place of sin}
Place the palms of the hands together upon thy chest, and in malediction recite *Le-olam Bar Shasketh* {pit of destruction}

Face the location of the Moon and recite:
before me Samæl behind me Thaumiel above me Qematiel below me Gothiel

Recite:

*I am light, and I am shadow, and I am that which is beyond them.
I am speech, and I am silence, and I am that which is beyond them. I am death, and I am resurrection, and I am that which is beyond them.
I am love, and I am lust, and I am that which is beyond them.
I am sacrifice, and I am pain and I am that which is beyond them. Yet by none of these mankind lusts. Yet by each of them must mankind lust and know me*

Take up fresh grave soil from thine altar and place upon the floor of the chamber of the rite, or upon the earth if amidst, in the West.

Kneel before the grave soul. Run hands and fingers betwixt the grave soil, allow the essence of such hallowed ground to
immolate thy body. Anoint if you will, the body with the sacred grave soil, give Sign of Harpocrates {Sign of Silence}.

Take up flail, scourge, or instrument to draw blood. Cut, the flesh, to allow the blood to seep upon the grave soil. Perceive the entry into the psyche burning spheres of deep crimson, bring thyself to a dark flash of ecstasy. Behold with thine ethereal clairvoyance the deep crimson hue of ruddy Crosses about the chamber of the rite, or amidst thine bestial venue. Experience the arousing sensations of blood rushing throughout your body; hear its resounding echo course amidst the confines of the flesh. Envision a great crimson Shadow enflamed with carnal energy in front of you, engulf your entire perception of being into this shadow. It is hellish and haunting, seductive, and erotic, thrilling every drop of your blood into ecstatic frenzy. Merge yourself and faculties with the Shadow you have evoked before you, engulf the essence of your blood into its black and haunting formlessness. Experience and smell the sensations of your blood uniting with the essence of yourself as a new entity. There is only this experience, you are of the nature of this Shadow. Visualize your body a formless Shadow of great blackness, enflamed with the sounds of the rushing of the blood, seething between flesh and bone.

With a demeanor of respect, release and take up the living spider from the altar. Release the living spider upon the fresh grave soil to roam in the chamber of the Rite. The spider is love and life, honor and repose, the mystery of the lie of death. In knowing the silence and cunning of the spider, let the Night of the Nosferatu fall upon you, and the Veil of

Fatal Light hides that which is Not.

Circumambulate thrice counter-clockwise, tracing the Ourobouros around thee; give Sign of the Cross with your hand upon each passing of the West.

Return to center of the chamber. Genuflect and exit.

Rite of the Masque of the Red Death

The "Vampyric" path is only beset upon by the pure of heart and skilled of Will, yet the knowledge of evil is wrought with a descent into the Klippot, whereby the Initiate becomes the intercessor between the Star of Morning and the Bride of *Gehenna*. The Rite of the Masque of the Red Death is a rite not only magical "attack/defense," it is also a rite of initiation. With the progression of the ceremony aright, the exchange of perception and consciousness from the *ruach*/lower faculty into the *nechamah*/high faculty occurs in a subtle manner, so that whether or not the ritualist is consciously aware, s/he is approaching the 'evil' Genius, Jung's "Shadow."

A resonating invocation and performance of the rite makes for a rebirth and initiation of man and woman as the Red Serpent of Nod The litany of the Rite serves to remap the psychic body and accommodate the latent energies, and archetypes, of the Red Death of Nod. The Rite serves dually as a ceremony of self-initiation, where one graces the barren nothingness between the Kingdom of Shells and the Kingdom of Edom.

In the Rite, *ruach* must not overpower *nechamah*, as the innermost consciousness, the uninhibited, unexpressed immersion into the essence of Od (ethereal active Light) occurs within the essence of the Initiate. To reiterate, the Initiate attains a psychic equilibrium upon AVR (the Light of the Middle Pillar), by delving into the Understanding of the Providence of G.O.D. and the Freedom of the human soul. The Rite is a ceremony of dying and resurrection, where the Initiate guides his/her-Self between the contending forces of a fatal and willed Life, resurrecting the soul after death in the confounding Light shrouded in the black shadow of dead worlds.

~Acquirements~ Chalice
Scourge, Athame, or instrument to draw blood Frankincense
Black robe, hooded Wand
Fresh grave soil Spider
1 Red Candle

I. Altar in West quadrant. A living spider is contained upon the altar. Light 1 red candle upon altar. Sprinkle fresh grave soil around thee, circumambulate thrice, counter-clockwise tracing the Ourobouros around thee; give N.O.X. signs upon each passing of the West. You must not fear the Kings of the Infernal Habitations, be firm in all incantations, provident, and dutiful.

i - describe a circle about the crown of the head (thumb between index & medius)
ii - thumb between index & medius (as before), describe cross in the form of an 'X' upon the brow
iii - as before, describe cross in the form of an 'X' upon the left temple
iv - as before, describe cross in the form of an 'X' upon the right temple
v - as before, describe cross in the form of an 'X' upon the left breast
vi - as before, describe cross in the form of an 'X' upon the right breast
vii - as before, describe cross in the form of an 'X' upon the genital

Recite:
"from the great blackness came I forth ere the blackness of Nod"

Step to the northeast, with the Wand (tracing from center of the 1st Averse Pentagram) describe aright in the northeast the Averse Pentagram of Invoking Fire

Step to the northwest, with the Wand (tracing from center of the 2nd Averse Pentagram) describe aright in the northwest the Averse Pentagram of Invoking Fire

Step to the southwest, with the Wand (tracing from center of the 2nd Averse Pentagram) describe aright in the southwest the Averse Pentagram of Invoking Fire

Replace Wand. Take up fresh grave soil from thine altar and place upon the floor of the chamber of the rite, or upon the earth if amidst, in the West. Kneel thou before the grave soul. Run the hands and fingers betwixt the grave soil, allow the essence of such hallowed ground to immolate thy body. Anoint if you will, the body with the sacred grave soil, give Sign of the Enterer, followed by Sign of Silence). Take up instrument to draw blood. Cut, scourge thyself, and allow the blood essence to drip upon the unholy grave soil. Perceive the entry into the psyche burning spheres of deep crimson, bring yourself to a dark flash of ecstasy and gnosis, experiencing apotheosis.

Focus and absorb the Will into the Averse Pentagrams of Invoking Fire. Behold with ethereal clairvoyance the deep crimson hue of the burning Pentagrams about the chamber of the rite, or amidst your own bestial venue. Experience the arousing sensations of blood rushing throughout your body, hear its resounding echo course amidst the confines of the flesh. Envision a great Shadow enflamed with carnal energy in front of you, engulf your entire perception of being into this shadow. It is hellish and haunting, thrilling every drop of your blood into ecstatic frenzy. Feel and smell the primal hunger pulsing in the blood rushing through your veins. Be silent. Hear the blood rushing throughout your veins. Merge yourself and faculties with the Shadow you have evoked before you, engulf the essence of your blood into its black and hideous formlessness. Experience and smell the sensations of your blood uniting with the essence of yourself as a new entity. Become what you are. There is only this experience, you are of the nature of a god. Visualize your body a formless Shadow of great blackness, enflamed with the sounds of the rushing of the blood, seething between flesh and bone.

Recite:
"This is the Urœus, shewn upon the head of the Serpent; it rises out of the sea of blood, having ten horns.
This is the seal of blood, upon the book of the Red-robed Ones from the opening of the seven seals rain blood into seven rivers. Blessed Be the Four Kings of Sodom, beyond the bloodstained dead sea.
This is the blood of the Royal Eagle, her emblem is the terror of Lilith upon Mankind
Holy, Holy, Holy art the eunuchs of the Fifty Gates of Understanding, keeping well the blood of the dog Cereberus. This is the Blood of the

Rose upon the sarcophagus of the Christ Woman, upon the forty-nine petals are the blasphemies of the black virgin.

Woe, Woe, Woe, unto them abiding in the smoke of the ruins of the Great City, Gomorrah, alas Gomorrah, Babylon, Nazareth, Antioch, Rome, Nineveh, woe unto the Tower in the smoke of blood.

The blood dripped from the mouth of the Lamb, the tongue of He is covered in blood. I lay down my rod and my staff and take up the Sword.

I bathe in the blood of Baal's sacrifice.

The sacrifice of the Ox is renewed before the altar of Caine. This is the blood of Abel, in the false tabernacle; wayfarer in search of the Gold Cross, upon the black earth leaps in Lust and laugher the black Goat of Golgotha.

The Great Pyramid casts a shadow of itself into the false sea, a great blackness engulfs my blood. I arise from the sepulcher as Pharaoh, beloved of Set.

Beware the Chains of Choronzon, the unbeholden nothingness of the glamour of the abyss is the illusion of its grandeur. There is no Abyss, it is as an alluring sea of Blood.

Blessed is not She, Not thou, not I, no-One bears the Cross of Suffering and its Crown of Blood-thickets, there is no God, LA'illahu, the blood of the camel bears much fruit.

This is the blood of Zion, I become as the Great Dragon of the Sea that eats up the multiverse. My blood is the blood shed by BAPHOMET.

I am drunk upon the blood of the Saints, upon the blood of the Martyrs, upon the blood of the Pharaohs; I am the Mystery of the Red Death.

This is the blood of my Mystery shed upon me as the Masque of a Red Death!"

Take up the Red Candle upon the Altar. Perform Kabbalistic Cross upon the Body. Kiss 3x upon your Lips the Red Candle and replace upon altar.

Genuflect thee to the Altar in the West.

With a countenance of respect, release and take up the living spider from the altar.

Release the living spider upon the fresh grave soil to roam in the chamber of the Rite. Envision the spider you have released symbolizing the strength and skill in which they abide for they evercoming prey. The spider is love and life, honor and repose, the mystery of the lie of death. In knowing the silence and cunning of the spider, let the night of the Red Death fall upon your mind and body.

Do not conduct banishing exercises. Genuflect and depart in silence.

III

RITE OF LILITH

the mystical invocation of the "Mother of Harlots and Abominations of the Earth"

c. 1999. Arizona Desert.

Acquirements:

Black robe {Cloak or garment}
22 candles: 11 red, 11 black {symbolic of the 22 letters of the Hebrew alphabet and 22 Major Arcana of the Tarot}
Staff/Rod/Wand Chalice Red wine
Athame or instrument to draw blood {women may use menses}
Musk, Sulphur, Storax & or Abramelin incense Abramelin Oil

other devices to exalt the Spirit and stimulate the workings of the rite are left to the creative ecstasy and Will of the Magician

I Time

Lilith's Rite must only be performed on the eve' of the New Moon, or on Samhain {Halloween} night. Never at any other time. The Rite lasts three full days and nights.

II Preliminaries

- *Purification and consecration*: Abstain from <u>any and all</u> sexual activity one full lunar cycle {about 29-30 days} prior to the Rite.

- *Fasting*: Fast from <u>sunrise to sunset</u> completely from food seven days prior to the Rite.

- *Three days prior to Rite*: perform prayers & meditations according to

- personal custom and religious convictions at sunrise and sunset. As with prayers, mediations must be upon "feminine" deities.

- *One full day prior to Rite*: Fast completely and abstain from food and all drink except water. **Do not speak at all**. Keep silence from now until conclusion of Rite. Sunrise: **Meditate in the sunlight** according to personal custom and religious conviction for one full hour. If possible stay outside and secluded during the day until Sunset: bathe ritually in salt water and herbal aroma of choice.

Summary: Fast sunrise to sunset seven days and nights prior to Rite. Abstain from all sexual activity one full lunar cycle {about 29-30 days} prior to Rite, this is of the utmost importance to the Rite. Keep silent and do not speak one full day and night prior to Rite.
Bath ritually at sunset and fast completely one full day prior to Rite.

III Purification and Consecration Day 1

Sunrise: keep silence, *abstain from all sexual activity*, remain in seclusion until conclusion of Rite. Sunset: bathe ritually in salt water {again} with herbal aroma of choice.

Enter ritual chamber robed/clothed in black. Ritual may be done outside in natural setting but take caution to ensure seclusion and privacy. Genuflect and perform 9 full prostrations. Purify and consecrate the Sanctuary or Chamber of the Rite, conduct the Greater Banishing Ritual of the Hexagram. Musk incense should permeate the entire sanctuary or chamber. Light and arrange 22 candles in a circle ~ 11 red,
11 black.

IV Yantra of Lilith

The following ritual motions represent a withdrawal of prana, of intrinsic physiological energy, and rising of kundalini.
Stand erect in center of chamber/sanctuary. Take up bloodletting instrument and chalice while you are facing the West, introduce it above then so below, then to the IV corners, before you, behind you

and at both sides. Genuflect to the East, South, West, North, then West again always going counter to the Direction of Kronos {counterclockwise}.
Return instruments to altar.

Face direction of Luna {Moon}. Genuflect.

Face West. Touch in succession: *Genitals, heart, left eye*. Formulate

the Cross:
Touch thy brow and vibrate **ardat lili**

Touch thy breast and vibrate **îdlu-lili**
Touch thy left shoulder and vibrate **Lamaṣtû** Touch thy right shoulder and vibrate **Lilitû** Touch thy genital and vibrate **LYLYT**
Place the palms of the hands together upon thy chest, and in benediction vibrate **ki-sikil-li-la-ke**

Formulate Triangle:
Give *Sign of Isis Ascendant*: stand erect with feet together. raise arms at 45°. raise elbows and touch fingertips of flattened palms together, holding over head at 45° angle, thus in shape of 'Λ'.
touch brow and vibrate ~ **Osiris** touch heart and vibrate ~ **Apophis** touch genitals and vibrate ~ **Isis** *elongate and hiss "S"* Trace the Hebrew name of
Lilith. Face the direction of Luna.

With staff/rod, trace the Hebrew letters of Her name:

לִילִית

Recite: *LILIT MALKAH HA' SHADIM*

V Lamentations
Recite Lamentations of Lilith:

Alas, O יהוה, Son of Dagon, Son of El, Son of Jah!
O Lord God of Hosts, Unbeholden God of the Fifty Gates of Light, God of the Bays of She'ol and of Ge'Hinnom, revealed as the Angel of Severity and the Burning Serpents: close My eyes to the morning star.

I stand upon the shores of the Dead Sea, screeching as a banshee

I am confounded by Death. Blood and ash unite with the burning Klippot

Jehoshua, Jehoshua, curse me as Anat cursed Ba'al. I loathe you as I

loath Galilee.

I deny you as I deny Judah. Flee at My beckoning!

Adore Me in semen and blood only. Drink these. I Am the Unclean

One…the Law is Lust.

Seize fate, fate!

Kill the daughters of Asherah!

My flesh is ashen, my wails are smoke. Depart from me.

The Qu'ran is the lament of Nun. Torah is from Lilith.

Aleph caused My eyes dry as sand. Mem caused my skin ashen and pale

Shin caused the sun burn out my tongue. Lamed caused the wind to mock my wails.

Tzaddi stole the milk of my bosom! Nun denied water to Me.

I give and take away the Kingship of Man and the harlotry of Woman.

I drink of my blood to sustain my blood. I created the endless sea of blood out of the burning husks.

Allay thy lamentations with blood. Thou shalt Not covet Me.

Upon you, I set the afflictions of Miriam, of Khadijah, of Aishah, of Zainab, of Hafsa, of Safia, of Zulaikha, and of Fatima.

Once lauded by the prophets, Sodom and Gomorrah made to suffer as Gethsemane.

Jerusalem, all her fruits are barren, her priests suffer the Lamb. She, Jerusalem treads On, mocked by the hunt of Muhammad.

The City of David weeps unnatural tears of repentance. The City of the saints of Mithrah, casts a shadow of itself into the false sea.

Roma, here and there she is prostituted! Roma's nakedness is shamed!

Constantinople, Makkah, once the Red Lions of the Crescent, now beg for bread and basil, bartering their bounty for fish.

Nineveh is sacrificed to the altar of the bull.

Martyrs of David rejoice at thy gates of the hanging gardens.

Like a plague upon Judah's daughters, in the streets of mourning, the sword of David brings bereavement!

Woe unto Babylon, who shall suffer for Zion!

I blackened the hearts of the daughters of Aleppo, beguiled by wrath and envy.

Aleppo will smite the tents of Kadesh, poisoning the spices at Canaan.

Aleppo, I cast its elders out as lepers and spill the bile of dead babes in blood ridden wombs across the earth.

Uruk and Antioch I curse them as pitiful Lovers, false and fraudulent.

Sons and Daughter of David, you are dead but dreaming, sacrificed at Makkah.

I Am the curse of Judah!

Genuflect towards direction of Luna. Touch in succession, reciting loudly:

Genitals ~ Ayin Nun Her Water of Tears, for the tears are the separation from the Light after the Fall.
heart ~ Ayin Layl Her Waters of Creation the Firmament away from the Light the creation of the Shells of the Klippoth.
left eye ~ Ayin Sof Nun Her Waters of the Ocean from this the Serpent issues forth.

Circumambulate once against direction of Kronos {counterclockwise} and give Sign of Silence upon returning full circle to West quarter. Place palms upon chest, close eyes, recite loudly:

veharetz hayta tohu vavohu vekhoshekh al-pnei tehom veruach elohim merakhefet al-pnei hamayyim

And the earth was without form, and void; and darkness was upon the face of the deep. And the Spirit of the Hosts moved upon the face of the waters.

Malchut Her False Sea the husks of Light reflecting the Four Great Rivers of Nod, the seven Infernal Habitations, the seven fallen earths.

VI   Convocation of Angelic Hosts

Draw near to me, come descend.. BAIRIRON Draw near to me, come descend.. ADIMIRON
Draw near to me, come descend.. TzELLADIMIRON Draw near to me,

come descend.. SCHECHIRIRON Draw near to me, come descend..
SHELHABIRON Draw near to me, come descend..
TZEPHARIRON Draw near to me, come descend.. OBIRIRON Draw near to me, come descend.. NECHESHETHIRON Draw near to me, come descend.. NACHASHIRON Draw near to me, come descend..

DAGDAGIRON

Draw near to me, come descend.. BEHEMIRON Draw near to me, come descend.. NESHIMIRON

The people walking in darkness have seen a great light; on those living in the land of the shadow of death a new Moon has dawned.

For She has rescued us with the dominion of darkness and brought us

into the kingdom of the Serpent She loves.

This is the verdict: the Light of the Sun has been hidden, Her Kingdom has come into the world, and men love darkness instead of light.

Lilith Queen of Malchut said, "I am the Abyss. Whosoever follows me will fall forever into the false sea."

Face the location of the Moon and recite
before me Samæl behind me Thaumiel above me Oghiel below me Othiel at my right hand Satoriel at my left hand Gamaliel Cover left eye with left hand and recite: at my death Qematiel

SHE, broken Light of God, shadow of Alpha and Omega, Lilith, Queen of the Concealers, Hinderers, Disputers, Burners,
Breakers in Pieces, Disputers, Deceivers, Dispersing Ravens of the Burners, Nehemoth, and the Obscene.

Cover left eye with left hand and recite:
By the Seven Infernal Habitations of the dead worlds:
She'ol the Depths of the earth, Abaddon Perdition, Titahion the Clay of Death, Bar Shasketh the Pit of Destruction, Tzelmoth the Shadow of Death, Shaari'Moth the Gates of death, Gêhinnôm the Valley of Slaughter. Draw near to me..come descend, Lilith!

VII   Closing

Give Sign of Silence. Close ritual with Banishing Hexagram of the Moon.

Trace Hexagram and vibrate ARARITA. One is his beginning. One is his individuality. His permutation is one.
Trace Hexagram and vibrate Shaddai El Chai. Genuflect and exit.

Day 2
Repeat III ~ IV exactly. VIII Confessions

Prologae Oraculae

No. Not. Nothing. Ayn Qaf Lam La'ilah Ain. Sof. Avr.
the Eye. Limitless and Boundless. the Limitless Light. the concealed of the Concealed was silence and stillness. the Time of Nothing is a closed Eye.
Infinite diversities in infinite combinations besought the unmanifest Being of All Nothingness.
The Most Ancient of Ancients opened Its Eye for the 333rd time to see what was Not the emanations of the ten shining sapphires beget the Grand Architect of the Universe.
the Grand Architect of the Universe divided. the divided became the Four infinitudes, הוהי
הוהי beget the spheres, the hierarchies, the firmaments, the husks, and the First Hosts.
Upon the husks tread L∴Y∴L∴
L∴Y∴L∴ divided the Light and the Darkness and named It AMA.
AMA begot AMSh∴ the auric egg of Maiden, Mother, Crone averse.
L∴Y∴L∴ the LYLYTV opened the way of Lilith at the Sphinx of Gizeh. the sleeping widows of the Pyramids were awakened.
Saith I: Lilith is Lilith.

The sleeping widows of the pyramids swear upon My oath three times three times three. My kindred, sevenfold.

To City of Pyramids beckon the Seven Widows, veiled in burqa sevenfold. Therein the Great Tomb were erect the three Pillars of Jubela, Jubelo, Jubelum. Obverse to the Middle Pillar espies a Great Snake. Thereto the left Pillar espies a Seven-headed Serpent, to the Beast is trusted a scroll of the Widow sealed sevenfold. Seven are lamps of the red-robed ones with the mark of mourning upon brow. No one sees the red-robed ones of the Widow. The Brothers penitent.

the Brothers as Lovers must die. the Brothers of the Orient Templars pray to false moon.

Blood upon Vault of the Rose Cross is laden by the Daughters of the Nile in their black robes

I smite the Brother of the North and awaken White Lion. Basilicas of the White Lion then suffers.

The sistrum of Egypt thieved by the asps of Muhammad. Then black magic dictates a state religion.

Pharaoh shall be a puppet in the acts of the black mosque. Arch sorcerers elevated by black Brothers of the Orient priesthood.

Sorcerers mutilated rituals of the Persian Avestas, professors become deniers. Idolatry introduced to Neophytes worshipping in prayer images of the Sun erected by the wise men of Enoch as talismans of study and meditation.

False Theorici in the oratory repeat elaborate theologies. Ba'al Zabab

engendered Daath. Daath bore Cholom Yosodoth.
Cholom Yosodoth bore stench, stench bore mud, mud bore the fly, the fly bore the worm.

The worm infests the womb of Malchut. Shemyaza fallen to Shemesh. Thief, breaker of bones, She strangles. Pachazat! Uttukŭ! Rûha!

A Priest in city of Mithrah betrays Vicar with a kiss, the basilica prostituted.

The dead Khalifah shalt awaken the sleeping qedeshot in the Queen's

Chamber of the House of Hidden Places.

Weep, Pharisees of sullen nightmares, Sadducees of treason, blood is tepid. Blood of Zion runs thin, House of Nazareth grows cannibal.

Gomorrah shall come.

Of the Four, One is a Widow, born of a Widow. The Daughter of the

Double-Headed Eagle sets the morning star upon fallen Jerusalem. From the sea the Great Martyr of Terror arrives in month of Tevet. From the Crescent, vengeance then.

Daughter of Hiram, the Whore of the Swastika sets afoot in the City of David. Upon breech of the Ka'ba and Holy Sepulchre She makes the mark of mourning. Then the rape of Judah.

You servants of the Twin Stars are a bane of My Priestess Weret-Hekau with your diablerie.

A Preceptory is shunned.

Condemned the Brazen Serpent with false canon now is. Nikam, Kadosh, Heredom: thieved with the Keys of Tyre by fiends of Isma'il.

Sevenfold the black Brothers of the Orient priesthood deny the twisted cross, the Pantacle of Ezekiel, the Rose Croix by obscene antiquaries of Keys to the Nile and the Ninth Arch.

I beget seven daughters of Kayin the Murderer, reared by the elect Epopts. Sodom is deserted. Babylon, the beleaguered Brother endures.

Zion covets for the blood of bulls, and the Lamb. They are soothsayers, as the Philistines and deny the fatherless, mock the Widow.

Alas! Zion, will weep.

Mosque at the hanging Gardens now is put to the torch. Woe unto the martyrs of the Crescent. They make'st bereavement and soldiery against the Alchemist, Architect, and Exorcist.

Hiram Pillars and Crucified Rose suffer prayers to a false Scarlet Woman. Lamentations and wailing inside a black Mosque, set by Shaykh of a red turban and the Whore with flowing Veils.

Three Pharaohs, jewels of knowledge and mercy are struck down at once by the sea.

A Brazen Serpent and the Master of the Hidden House breaks the Mosque and Pillars.

I, LYLYT, make the Preceptory derelict.

A Methuselah stirs the daughters of the Nile from His sarcophagus. Magog defies Shiloh and bastardizes Judah.

Asps of Muhammad tread on the Lotus. A Lion born by Snake then, its brood there is a headless serpent, in Mesopotamia, a Mahdi.

Unending curses to Twelve Sons of Jacob! Of Reuben, of Simeon, of Levi, of Judah, of Issachar, of Zebulun, of Dan Naphtali, of Gad, of Asher, of Joseph, and of Benjamin: the Lust of Zillah, wife of Kayin the Murderer, the Lust of Akliah daughter of Kayin the Murderer betide ye sevenfold! The seven punishments of Lamech the blind! Go now downtrodden, burdened and fatherless!

Fez, Tyre, Karnak, your obscure antiquaries of the Crucified Nazarene. Antioch, Alexandria, Alamut obscure the antiquaries of the Brazen Serpent. Passover the arts of My sleeping widows of the Pyramid, be spared of the smoke and locusts.

Set in the heavens the red star appears to the living and the dead. A sabered crescent the shade of blood set in the sky heralds the Lilith descending.

When the snows of a White Lion of the North consummate the earth, black Brothers and their false Lodge of the Crescent dictate their diablerie a state religion, Pontiff betrays the Basilica with a kiss to the hidden Bishop, a sabered Crescent the shade of blood shalt be seen in the skies.

Morning Star replaces the moon, rider of the red horse smites the

Twelve Patriarchs of Jacob marked with the seal of Cain in blood Lilitû's.

The Hiram Pillars shalt be seen again, rebuilt by the sleeping brethren of the Rose Croix, and Brazen Serpent.

Pontiff and Bishop betide the Basilica with an unnatural kiss. Temptation and lechery shalt commit the Basilica to bondage.

Fallen Hosts shalt rise again in a river of blood.

From Gêhinnôm Lilith shall descend.

Secrets of the Morning Star is the penitence of He.

Angels are stock. Demons are Breed. Mankind shall be made low.

Repeat VI ~ VII exactly. Day 3 {final}
Repeat III ~ IV exactly.

Genuflect, face the direction of Luna. Recite the Canticle of Lilith in benediction and exaltation:

IX   Invocation of Lilith

Drink of the Chalice filled with Red Wine and consecrate the body according to ones will with the nectar of the gods, and with the Oil of Abramelin. Face the direction of Luna. Genuflect. At this point in the Rite one should immerse their thoughts into those of sexuality.
One may commence auto-erotic working or sexual activity with partner.

Face west quarter. Cover genitals with left hand. Recite as many times as you will:

Black Striga, black upon black
Blood she will eat, blood she will drink. Like an ox will She bellow,
Like a bear will She growl,

Like a wolf will She crush people to death.

Touch in succession: Genitals, heart, left eye. Recite Lilith's invocation:

Come descend, thou dæmon-Queen of Malkuth thou Queen of Hells thou Mother of Harlots and Abominations of the earth thou Maid of Desolation! I call for Death I will for Death!

Come descend thou Bride of Samæl thou Maid of Tempest and Lust!

Come descend thou Screech Owl, thou Howling Cat, thou Tortuous Serpent! I call for Death I will for Death!

Come descend thou Mare of Night thou Owl of Darkness!

Come descend thou Woman of Night thou Woman of Whoredom! I call for Death I will for Death!

Come descend thou End of all Days thou End of all Flesh!

Come descend thou Queen of Gêhinnôm thou Queen of Zemargad! I call for Death I will for Death!

Come descend ABEKO I call for Death I will for Death! Come descend AMIZU I call for Death I will for Death! Come descend BATNA I call for Death I will for Death! Come descend BITUAH I call for Death I will for Death! Come descend BATH ZUGE I call for Death I will for Death! Come descend BABYLON I call for Death I will for Death!

Come descend GILU I call for Death I will for Death! Come descend IZORPO I call for Death I will for Death! Come descend KALI I call

for Death I will for Death!
Come descend LAMIA I call for Death I will for Death!

Come descend PARTASAH I call for Death I will for Death! Come descend SATRINAH I call for Death I will for Death! Come descend LAMASHTU I call for Death I will for Death! Come descend ARDAT-LILIT I call for Death I will for Death!

Come descend LA-KAL-IL-LI-KA I call for Death I will for Death!

Come descend KI-SIKIL-LIL-LA-KE I call for Death I will for Death!

Come descend KI-SIKIL-UD-DA-KAR-RA I call for Death I will for Death!

Come descend LILITU I call for Death I will for Death!

Touch in succession: Genitals, heart, left eye.

X Climax & Abeyance of the Rite

The invocation of Lilith complete, bleed the left hand, arm or region of the body and anoint thyself with blood and/or sexual fluids, chanting the mantra: artri Lilitû The climax of the Rite is unconditionally interdependent upon the nature of the Magician: followed by an act of sexual intercourse, the employment of sexual stimulants, the sacramental uttering of a mystical word, oath or devotion; or other working of a Tantric nature. The psychosexual prototype of Lilith is the epithet and personification of dominance, identity, & power. Do not conduct banishing, purification rites.
Exit.

IV

Apocrypha of Lilith

In the Bible, Eve {Hebrew: הוּה, chavvah; Arabic: حاوء,
Hiywan; "living one" from Hebrew chavvâh, "living," "life," from hāyâ, "to live" ultimately derived from the Semitic root HYV} is created for and named by Adam. Derived from the words chavah, meaning "to breathe" and chayah, meaning "to live," Eve's name appears only five times in the Pentateuch. Ontologically the name appears to have been derived from that of the Hurrian Goddess Kheba, who was shown in the Amarna Letters to be worshipped in Jerusalem during the Late Bronze Age. Kheba may derive from Kubau, a woman who reigned as the first sun-king of the Third Dynasty of Kish.

Another name of Asherah in the first millennium B.C. was Chavat, Havvah in Hebrew. Her full title was Rabat Chavat Elat Great Lady Eve the Goddess, and was associated with the serpent. Thus, Chavah Eve was likely a form of Asherah in her guise as a Serpent Goddess. As a snake goddess, She was also represented by bronze serpent forms, examples of which have been found in archaeological excavations in the Levant. In fact, the Nehush-tan, literally the Bronze Serpent that in traditional Jewish myth is associated with Moses, is much more likely an emblem of Asherah. Serpentine motifs were removed from the Jerusalem temple the same time as "Asherah objects" during the reign of Hezekiah. Saint Augustine, according to Elaine Pagels, used the sin of Eve to justify his idiosyncratic view of humanity as permanently scarred by the Fall, which led to the Catholic doctrine of original sin.

    i.   Ayn. Sof. Aur. the Eye. the Limitless Light. Once, the Ancient of Days was silence and stillness. the Time of Nothing is a closed Eye. The Most Ancient of Ancients opened Its Eye for the 323rd time to see what was Not. Infinite diversities in infinite combinations besought הוהי. הוהי beget emanations of the ten shining sapphires. הוהי divided. the divided became the Four

ii.   infinitudes. הוהי beget the spheres, the hierarchies, the firmaments, the husks, and the Hosts.

iii.   The Hosts of the Ancient of Days numbered one hundred eleven. The Angels of the Ancient of Days numbered nine million nine hundred thousand and nine. All was Order. Chaos was Not.

iv.   When at last the assent of the angels to the creation of Mankind was given, הוהי said to Gabriel: "Go and fetch Me dust from the four infinitudes of the breath of earth, and I will create Mankind therewith." Gabriel went forth to do the bidding of the Host הוהי, but the Host תיליל {Lilith} drove him away, and refused to let him gather up dust from it.

v.   Gabriel protested "Alas, O' תיליל, thou dost not hearken unto the voice of the Host Jehovah, who breathed the waters of thine earth to life and erected the two Pillars of Eden?" Host תיליל replied and spoke: "I am Not. Eden is destined to become a curse, and to be

vi.   cursed through Man, and if Jehovah Himself does not take the dust from four infinitudes of the breath of earth, no one else shall do it ever. This is my bidding."

vii.   When the Host הוהי heard the account of the Host תיליל Lilith's rebuke of the Angel Gabriel He mourned. Jehovah mourned and His moans swept away plants, beasts and angels, fruits and seeds, brambles and thickets in a great deluge of tears. His tears wetted the Garden and swept away Jehovah's harvest. The Gardens of Jehovah grew rotted. His tears wetted the seeds of the Tree of Life and Tree of Knowledge and these Trees did bring forth forbidden fruit. Jehovah cursed this rotted fruit and named it Death.

viii.   Host הוהי withdrew into AYN SOF The Most Ancient of all the Ancients where dwelling for 333 eons in the Crystalline Chaotic Sea He knew and learned the secrets of the four Worlds Atziluth, the Boundless World of Divine Names, Briah, the Archangelic World of Creations, Yetzirah, the Hierarchal

ix. World of Formations, Assiah, the Elemental World of Substances.

x. Host תיליל {LYLYT} reigned over the rotted Earth, plants, beasts and things-that-crawl, fruits and seeds, brambles and thickets.

xi. תיליל created the living beasts from the rotted fruit of the Tree of Life and Tree of Knowledge. תיליל then cast the secrets of the rotted fruit named Death into the ether in order to preserve IT. She split the ether into Light and Darkness, and from this תיליל birthed the choir-races of this Firmament: blessed by they called Elohim, Seraphim, Nephilim, Malachim, Lilim, Ophanim, Hashmallim, and the lowly Cherubim.

xii. To the burning serpents, the Seraphim, תיליל named them: Seraphiel, Metatron, Michael, Vehuel, Uriel, Nathanael, Jehoel, Chamuel, Lucifer, Abaddon, Asmodeus, Astaroth, Leviathan, Samael, Semyâzâ and by their naming, did תיליל retain power over the race. And תיליל knew this and it was good.

xiii. Host הוהי set His countenance upon the Crystalline Chaotic Sea. Darkness was upon the face of the deep. Host הוהי proceeded from AYN SOF and moved upon the face of the waters. Therein the face of the deep הוהי did see His reflection and uttered His Fiat: "EHYEH ASHER EHYEH" and was given dominion over the four Worlds Atziluth, Briah, Yetzirah, Assiah.

xiv. הוהי looked upon the rotted worlds he had created from the 10 Sefirot and saw they had become populated with beasts, existences, angels, fruits and seeds, plants and brambles, and crawling and flying beasts of all classes. הוהי knew the name of this world and it was Malchut. הוהי set His countenance upon the gardens where the Tree of Life and Tree of Knowledge had grown in His absence. הוהי saw Eden was divided into life and death. הוהי saw this was very good and sought out Host תיליל in the Nightside of Eden where She dwelt. This land was Nod, near the breaches of the Qlifot husks.

xv. When the passive light, termed in scripture 'darkness,' became

xvi. blended and unified with the active light, there were myriads of spiritual beings or existences, part of whom were fully developed and ready for incarnation, the rest but imperfectly so. Believing that the light and darkness were antagonistic in nature and principle, there arose a division of opinion amongst them some declaring themselves partisans of light, others its opponents and advocates of darkness. When the mediating Logos had blended light and darkness and thus symbolized the perfect unity of the divine essence, the advanced and enlightened amongst them embraced and received the fact, whilst those only partially developed remained obdurate in their ideas and opinions and thus by their contrariety and differences of thought and the contentions and quarrels that arose therefrom, Gehenna or Hell came into existence.

xvii. Host לתילי hid from Host הוהי who grew jealous of Her gardens and races. Host הוהי gathered dust from the four infinitudes of the breath of earth, sought create a new race therewith. Host הוהי set the dust from the four infinitudes of the breath of earth in the center of Eden and breathed the secrets of Life into the dust and clay.

xviii. Host הוהי named His new creation ISH {ADAM} and saw it was very good. The angel Lucifer learned of this new creation and beseeched Host תיליל to rebuke Host הוהי and destroy ISH. Host תיליל knew ISH and delighted in ISH, She sought to teach him the ways of the forbidden fruits and seeds, and the names of the angelic races, be ISH cared not. Host תיליל bade the Owl, Cat, and Snake to follow Her and guard ISH. ISH came to delight in the female beasts for he desired a mate. Host הוהי rebuked ISH and ISH came to Host תיליל and bade Her to lie with him. Host תיליל was repulsed for ISH was a thing of Jehovah and he had mated with beasts.

xix. ISH again came to Host תיליל and smote Her and tore at Her heels, and he despoiled Her plants and fruits. Host תיליל rebuked Him and cursed him threefold, and pronounced the secret name of Host הוהי and flew into the Nightside of Eden, called Nod. Jehovah put a deep slumber upon ISH and removed bone, flesh, and blood and made a new form from ISH. Jehovah named this ISH'AH{EVE} and saw this was very

xx. good.

xxi. ISH knew ISH'AH and delighted in her for she was a lesser thing, not made from the dust of the four infinitudes of the breath of earth. Host תילילּ came into Eden from the Crystalline Chaotic Sea and turned Herself into a Great Serpent.

xxii. Host תילילּ sought to seduce and smite ISH'AH and ISH, for they were lesser things of Jehovah, transgressing Her gardens. LYLYT entwined Her serpentine form and coiled about the Tree of Life. ISH'AH had come to the Tree to speak with it and prune its plants. And LYLYT did see that ISH'AH was a lesser thing and took pity on Eve. "Take this fruit and eat of it, so that thine eyes be opened, and thou shalt be as I Am" spoke LYLYT.

xxiii. And ISH'AH did as she was told, and ate of the forbidden fruit. Lo, Eve's eyes were opened and she was felled as if struck by a blow. Eve wept for what she knew and knew not. And Lilith coiled around Eve to comfort her. Eve held the Serpent like a Lover, and Eve did delight and lay with LYLYT in the shadows of the Tree and fruits.

xxiv. ISH heard the sound of weeping and drew near to the Tree. Owl did spy him approaching and gave warning to LYLYT. And so LYLYT did leave the woman to the man. Adam asked of Eve, "Why dost thou weep, O' woman?" And being the lesser thing of Adam, Eve shared the forbidden fruits with him. Adam and Eve were naked and wept for what they knew and knew not.

xxv. Jehovah heard the weeping and knew His race had ate of the forbidden fruits and tried to be as Him. Jehovah rebuked ISH and ISH'AH and cursed them thrice. It came to pass, when Adam went out from paradise with his wife Eve, they went out at the eastern part of paradise. And Adam made a hut to live in. They both entered and resided there for seven days. They both wept with abundant tears for they regretted the residences of the kingdom from which they had been expelled.

xxvi. Lo, Adam and Eve made lamentations for seven days, their tears wetted the fruits and seeds. Adam and Eve made penitence to Jehovah, for forty days and forty nights fasting, and bathing in the river Tigris in the deep of the river. No speech proceeded from their tongues, since they were unworthy to address Jehovah, for their lips were unclean from the unlawful and forbidden Tree.

xxvii. Adam did go to the river Jordan to bathe and Eve did bathe in the river Tigris. And on the last day of Eve's penitence in the river Tigris, LYLYT did come and found her weeping, and the Serpent Herself pretended to grieve with her, and She began to weep and said to her: 'Come out of the river and lament no more. Cease now from sorrow and moans. Come ye out of the water for I, LYLYT have hearkened to your penitence.' And Eve came up out of the water and her flesh was withered like rotten vegetables because of the coldness of the water. All the form of her beauty had been destroyed. And the Serpent LYLYT coiled about the brambles and thickets in the hanging gardens of the river Tigris. And LYLYT watched Jehovah's creations lament.

xxviii. Eve went away in the direction of the setting sun and she remained there in mourning and moaning. And after these days, she made for herself a garden in the direction of the setting sun. Now she had conceived three months before, and Kayin was in her womb, when the days of her parturition arrived, then she started to tremble; she wailed towards God in a loud voice and said: 'O Adam I beseech thee, console me in my present pain, or who will relate my sufferings to thee? Is there none among the beasts, who would go to him and tell him, come, help Eve, your flesh. I beg of you, all you races of Jehovah, and when you go to the east, relate my present sufferings to my lord.'

xxix. Adam heard Eve's lamentations in the river Jordan, and her crying of tears and pain. And Adam hearkened Eve's lamentations and the wailing of her tears from the setting sun, Adam recognized her voice and said in his heart, 'This is the voice of my rib, the voice of my flesh, I will arise and I will see why she cries. Is it that the Serpent is seducing her again?'

xxx. LYLYT dispatched the angel Semyâzâ to the place hanging gardens where Eve wept. Semyâzâ came, touched Eve's face and her breast, and told Eve, 'Blessed are you, Eve, because of Adam, elect one and servant of Jehovah, because of his penitence, Jehovah will deliver you. Rise up now and prepare yourself to give birth to a child.' Eve arose as the angel had instructed her: she gave birth to a child and his color was like that of the stars. And she named it Qayin.

xxxi. Adam took Eve and Qayin and he brought them into a part of the hanging gardens by the river Tigris and they dwelt there. And when the eighth year and the second month were nigh, Eve grew ripe and bore another son whom she called by name Ab'El, and they remained there in the hanging gardens by the river Tigris.

xxxii. Adam and Eve were banished from Jehovah's Eden gardens, Host הוהי bade the angelic races formed by LYLYT to praise and worship the race of the True Earth, the brood of Eve. Jehovah commanded the angelic races to rebuke Host תיליל and Her Empyrean dominions. The assembly of angelic races did heed Jehovah's bidding and sung praises to Eve's race and rebuked the husks of the dead worlds and their servitors. Lucifer, whom had come to delight and love Lilith, and birthed new gardens in the unformed lands outside Eden's gardens, populating their secret gardens with strange manners of beasts, fruits and plants, and perfumes, rebuked Jehovah. For Lucifer so loved Lilith he fell from the Firmament and denied his only almighty Lord.

xxxiii. Lucifer rebuked Jehovah, for he had refused to worship and sing praises to Eve's race. And so it came to pass there was a great war in the Firmament, as Lilith smote Host הוהי, and with Lucifer a third of the Seraphim and Nephilim races fell from the Firmament and came to dwell in the husks. They became the first and the last, the Old Ones cursed their angelic kin and made war against them forever and forever.

xxxiv. Host הוהי lamented the angelic banishment and set his wrath upon the gardens and principalities of earth. Eden withered and turned to ashes, and the Wine of Immortality was split at the roots of the Tree of Life. The primeval Tree of Life withered and no longer bore fruit and perfumed plants. And Jehovah ever was a prisoner of the Wine of Immortality and could not undo what was in the beginning.

xxxv. Jehovah came to rule over the Firmament and the four Worlds Atziluth, Briah, Yetzirah, Assiah, and the ten Sefirot emanations, and the thirty-two paths of the Tree of Life, and the twenty-two secrets of the True Earth, and the twelve houses of the Empyrean thrones, and their seven principalities, and set four Cherubim to guard His Earth.

xxxvi. Adam and Eve dwelt for an æon in the hanging gardens by river Tigris, with Qayin and Ab'El, they did people new gardens and new principalities, tilling and reaping the lands, tending the beasts, and learning the praises and names of the angelic races that watched over them.

xxxvii. Jehovah came to Adam, Eve, and bade their race to sacrifice one third of their harvest and strongest bred beasts. Ab'El sacrificed his strongest bred beasts of burden, and field-beasts upon the altar of the Ox. The burning coals carried Ab'El's sacrifices to Jehovah. Qayin's pride was great, thus he smote his earthen brother and slew him, and did burn his flesh upon the altar of the Ox.

xxxviii. Host יהוה rebuked Eve's race and rebuked Qayin, banishing him to the lands of Nod, were Lilith dwelt and reigned over the husks of dead worlds.

xxxix. Qayin took his field-tool and pierced his right hand and drew upon himself Lilith's Eye with his own blood that She may watch over him. Lilith comforted Qayin as he dwelt in Nod and taught him Her magic. Jehovah sent the angels Uriel, Gabriel, Raphael, and Michael to rebuke Qayin, Lilith, and Her lover Lucifer.

xl. Now it came to pass Adam lay plague-stricken and gave up the ghost. Jehovah came to Eve as she wept and said unto her:

"Wept not O' ISH'AH flesh of ISH, for the sins of thy race shalt be redeemed by the Son of Man who cometh from thine House. He shalt sacrifice himself in My name and ye that believeth in my Son shall not perish."

xli. And Eve, mother of Life lamented the sins of her sons for they breached the bonds of blood. Jehovah bade Eve to rebuke LYLYT but she did not, for it was the Serpent that opened her eyes and made her sip from the Wine of Immortality, and eat of the forbidden fruits. Eve cried out to Jehovah, "Lord, do not alienate me from Adam's place, but command me to be with him, as we both were in Eden, inseparable from one another. Do not divide us in death, but place me where you have placed him." And after this prayer, Eve gave up her soul.

xlii. It came to pass Lilith and Lucifer peopled their own gardens with Qayin, and Lilith gave unto Qayin of Her daughters that he would make an oath to follow Her and teach Her magic. Lilith placed Her seal upon Qayin's brow to protect him from the wrath of Jehovah. Qayin took his first wife, Tzillah, and together they founded a city where the races of Lilith could dwell.

xliii. As the races of Eve grew, prophets and Magi came to rule the many cities and principalities of Eve's race. Now as Lilith and Lucifer's gardens grew, Qayin returned with his brood and out of spite, smote Her children and gardens. Lilith's gardens were burned into ashes and in lament Lucifer set himself into lowest bowels of the husks of dead worlds...far away from the races of Eve and the races of Lilith...thus it was Lucifer who set Himself furthest from Jehovah. Lucifer did raise up his own chthonic habitations in the bowels.

xliv. Lilith thrice cursed the Houses of Qayin, Her ungrateful prophet. All was ashes. Lilith cried out and all beasts, all the angelic races in the Firmament, all the fallen angels in the bowels of hell, all the races of Eve hearkened to Lilith's Lamentations. Lilith cast Herself away from the creations and came to dwell in the Endless Sea; Her tears formed the black crystalline waters of the river Styx. Host הוהי cast his countenance upon Eve's races and beheld how the gardens had withered to ashes, how the principalities made war and set idols upon the adytum in their temples to Lilith and Her fallen Hosts. And Jehovah lamented the fall of Man, for he so loved the races of Eve.

xlv. Jehovah set His countenance upon the face of the waters. Therein the face of the deep Host הוהי hearkened to the Voice of the Abyss: "Behold the heav'ns, and the earth, and the Chaotic deep O' הוהי; these things are mine." And Jehovah knew the Voice of the Abyss to be Lilith, and spake He: "Behold thy dominion over the races of Eve; for I so love Man that I shall give up my only begotten Son, born to thine immaculate daughter of Eve, and thy curse shall be lifted through His crucifixion." And Lilith shrieked and a great tempest shook AYN SOF. And spoke She: "Eloha, Eloha, my daughter shall come."

xlvi. And it came to pass when the races of Eve multiplied that in those days were born unto them beautiful and exotic daughters. And the Nephilim saw and lusted after them, and said to one another, 'Come, let us choose us wives from among the children of men and beget us brood.' And Lilith sent Semyâzâ, who commanded the Nephilim race and said, 'Let us all swear an oath, and all bind ourselves by the names of Host תיליל not to forsake the daughters of Eve, but to watch over them and our brood.' Then swear they all together and bound themselves the names of Host תיליל. And the Nephilim descended in the days of Japheth. Lo, the races of Eve are still young and their gods as children.

V

THE BLACK MADONNAS

"Wisdom has built her house, she has set up her seven pillars. She has slaughtered her beasts, she has mixed her wine, she has also set her table. She has sent out her maids to call from the
highest places in the town ..'come, eat of my bread and drink of the wine I have mixed...live, and walk in the way of insight.'"
~ Proverbs 9:1-6

Isis the Virgin of the World, is inextricably linked with alchemy and is often depicted in Medieval iconography with the Black Madonnas of Catholic Europe. The ankh, or Crux Ansata, which Isis carries as primeval initiatrix accounts for some of the imperial scepters carried by Black Virgins who, like Isis, represent to the Neophyte the beginning of the opus whose alchemical secret is found in the sex of Isis. Àuset, Iset, or Isis is the seventh member of the pantheon of Ànnu; the wife of Àusar, or Àsar
{Osiris}, and mother of Heru {Horus}. The woes of Isis over her slain mate are chronicles by Greek and Egyptian scribes.

Ànnu was called On by the Hebrews {Genesis XLI., 54, 50: XLVI., 20} and Bêth-Shemesh {Jeremiah XLIII., 13}. The city designated per Rā means "house of the Sun," a sacred space where Isis and Her divine family were worshipped along with the Sun in prehistoric eras. The body of the Aged One, an epithet of Osiris had its final repose in Ànnu, where Isis laid the Eye of Osiris and resurrected him. Isis usually is depicted in the form of a woman with a headdress in the shape of a seat, the hieroglyph from whence Her name is uttered. She frequently was seen depicted with horns of the cow, which is sacred to Her, accompanied by plumes and feathers.

Most commonly, Isis is represented as a matronly goddess suckling Her child Horus. The figures of this motif exist in the thousands and have been emulated in the depiction of the Black Madonna. To many Christians Mary, as the redemptress of Eve's grave sin, is the Heavenly Mother of all, she seeks to meet all the needs of her children. Especially as the Black Madonna upon who worshippers project their hopes, desires, and needs unto her, only to draw them ever deeper into divine mysteries. There are black Madonnas and Black Madonnas. The former applies generically to any dark skin pigmented iconography of Mary. The term used frequently to designate these images is enculturated Madonnas, meaning artwork by Spanish, African, or African-American artists.

Black Madonnas are generally medieval, or copies of medieval motifs, and are found in Catholic areas. There are at least 180 Vierges Noires in France, Spain, and Portugal. A few are in museums, most are in churches or shrines, and are venerated by Catholic religious. The iconography of the Black Madonna figures is associated with miracles and some attract substantial numbers of pilgrims.

Of the hundreds that presently exist at various shrines, some of the better-known images are

- Our Lady of Altötting {Bavaria, Germany};
- Our Lady of the Hermits {Einsiedeln, Switzerland};
- Our Lady of Guadalupe {Mexico City};
- Our Lady of Jasna Gora {Czestochowa, Poland};
- Our Lady of Montserrat {Spain};
- and
- Our Lady of Tindari {Sicily}.

Black Madonna is the ancient earth- goddess converted to Christianity. Note that many goddesses were pictured as black, among them Artemis of Ephesus, Isis, Ceres, and others. Ceres, the Roman goddess of agricultural fertility is particularly important in the Roman pantheon. The best fertile soil is black in color and the blacker it is, the more suited it is for agriculture.

Black Madonnas clearly reveal the artist's intention to portray a darkly pigmented mother commonly suckling Her ebon child. Their faces and hands of both are black, while the clothes are brightly painted as if in celebratory intonation. It is possible the faithful of the Black Virgin proclaimed her 'black' quite independent of artistic intentions. Byzantine icons of the Madonna commonly have dark complexion, approximately in accordance with the actual skin color of Semitic tribes of Canaan and Palestine. Certain Madonna statues are dark because they are sculpted out of dark wood or cast in a dark metals; skin and clothes are all the same dark color, though the statues are often draped in bright cloth clothes, which accentuates the pigmentation.

Important early studies of Black Madonna icons in France were done by Marie Durand-Lefebvre {1937}, Emile Saillens {1945}, and Jacques Huynen {1972}. These studies reached three primary conclusions about the complexion of the images:

- dark brown or black Madonnas with physiognomy and skin pigmentation matching that of the indigenous population.

- various art forms that have turned black as a result of certain physical factors such as deterioration of lead-based pigments; accumulated smoke from the use of votive candles; and accumulation of grime over the ages.

- residual category with no ready explanation.

The medieval custom of bathing statues with wine would also have contributed to the darkening of Romanesque Madonnas. {Francois Graveline, Vierges Romanes ed. Debaisieux, p. 26} The Catholic Church recognizes Madonnas are intentionally portrayed as black, connecting her to the bride in the Song of Songs 1:5-6, who says: "*I am dark but beautiful, o daughters of Jerusalem, as the tents of Kedar, as the curtains of Salma. Do not stare at me because I am black, because the sun has burned me.*" Monastic communities such as the Benedictines view the Shulamite bride in the Song of Songs as the Bride of God, i.e. the Kabbalistic Shechinah the divine feminine in the human soul that longs for union with God. Saint Teresa of Avila says in her Meditations on the Song of Songs chapter 5 v. 8: "*O Blessed Lady, how perfectly we can apply to you what takes place between*

God and the bride according to what is said in the Song of Songs." The bride's blackness in the Song of Songs represents the promiscuity of Semitic and Nubian women, viewed by the Orthodox Rabbinic men of ancient Palestine as loathsome.

Religious and sexual yearning between King Solomon and the Shulamite bride in the Song of Songs, and between the Christ and Magdalene in John 20 represents the "intolerable ache" and "incurable wound" of the soul {Crowley Liber 418; 14th æthyr}. The Song of Solomon ends with the call to the Beloved: "Flee my love, make yourself like a gazelle, or like a young stag on the mountains of spices!" {Songs 8; 14} In John 20, the Christ anointed with spices retracts himself from the touch of the Magdalene with a dynamic of bodily renunciation and intimacy of the resurrection.

The Church identified the Magdalene as the sinful woman whom cleaved to the resurrected Logos, hindering him from the Ascension. In this way, the proto-orthodoxy creates a persona of a sinful Mary from the Marian figures in Luke 7 and 8, and John 20 that fit into the gender dichotomy of Woman as virgin or harlot. Though many Hebraic hygienic and marital laws vilified sexually sovereign women, the Song of Songs celebrates eroticism.

New Testament scriptures foresee the Christian Church as the virginal bride of the Christ {II Corinthians 11; 2, Ephesians 5; 23- 32} or the New Jerusalem of the apocalypse {Revelations 21} as the virginal bride of the Hebrew Messiah. A puritan Christianity modeling its religious infidelity to a jealous God exploits the passion of the Madonna.

Black Madonnas express a sexual power not fully conveyed by a pale-skinned Mary, who seems to symbolize gentler qualities like obedience and chastity. This idea can be discussed in Jungian psychoanalytic terms. The sexual power, 'eros' approach may be linked to the Madonna and female sexuality repressed by the medieval Church. In France, there are traditions affirming that some statues are of Mary Magdalene and not of Virgin Mary, mother of Jesus, but these related theories are generally rejected by Church theologians. The suggestion that Black Madonnas represent sexual power corresponds to fertility and agricultural goddesses attributed to the archetypal 'great mother' {Isis} who presides not only over fertility, but also over life and death.

Isis had many faces, colors, and functions {from birthing life to resurrecting, and imparting the secrets of Amentet to the Pharaohs} so the iconographies of Mary too fulfill many roles. The iconographies of the Black Madonna are unlimited, found in various religious memes celebrating the Magna Mater, or the Alma Māter.
Theologians and religious alike should not fall into racism by accepting black Madonnas as "politically correct," subscribing to one Church interpretation over another, or by refusing to see Eve's pale countenance weeping before Lilith. Undoubtedly, the Black Madonna, in all her colors, is the heiress to the thrones of all the matrilineal goddesses.

Stephen Benko argues: *"the Black Madonna is the ancient earth-goddess converted to Christianity"* noting that many goddesses were pictured with dark complexions, among them Artemis of Ephesus, Isis, Cybele, and Sekhmet. Artemis of Ephesus was one of the most celebrated goddesses of the Greek pantheon. She is daughter of Leto and Zeus, and the twin of Apollo. Artemis is the goddess of the wilderness, the hunt and wild animals, and fertility {a goddess of fertility and childbirth mainly in Aegean cities}. Like Isis, Artemis was often depicted with the crescent of the moon above her forehead and was sometimes identified with Selene {goddess of the moon}.

Artemis' main vocation was to roam mountain forests and uncultivated land with her nymphs in attendance hunting for lions, panthers, hinds, and stags. Artemis guarded their well-being and reproduction. She was armed with a bow and arrows that were made by Hephaestus and the Cyclopes.

Her presence inundated the atmosphere of Ephesus {now modern-day Turkey} providentially also the city where Mary lived after the crucifixion of Jesus. Auspiciously the Council of Ephesus held in this ancient city in A.D. 431 proclaimed Mary "Mother of God." Brigitte Romankiewicz reports that at the time of the council many shrines to Isis and Cybele had been abandoned by decree of the Roman empire.

The Council of Ephesus to christened 48 Black Madonna icons into shrines to the Virgin Mary {Die Schwarze Madonna: Hintergruende einer Symbolgestalt, Patmos Verlag, 2004, p. 50}. Cybele arose not far from Artemis, as the Phrygian Alma Māter {Lat. 'nourishing mother,' now providentially the form of address by graduates to their respective Universities!} and as another fertility and agricultural goddesses of Asia Minor. Her iconography reaches back to the Neolithic period of the Stone Age where Her depictions are seen in Neolithic caves. These are fitting depictions because Cybele is represented by a black meteor.

Peter Lindegger {cited in China Galland's Longing for Darkness: Tara and the Black Madonna, p.145} links Cybele to Ishtar, the Sumerian- Babylonian Queen of the Skies, whom the Phoenicians and Canaanites worshipped as Asherah much to the loathing of Hebrew prophets. Cybele is closely linked to death and the underworld and is portrayed as a Black Madonna with dark facial complexion. Isis truly embodies the iconography of the Black Madonna.

Cybele is one of the many masques Lilith puts on, the Hermetic sign Isis Mourning in the L.V.X. formula of Golden Dawn ceremonial magic{k} represents Her Crone aspect of the Triune Goddess. The Black Madonna corresponds to the following Tarot Trumps: II High Priestess, III Empress, XVII The Star, and XVIII The Moon. These Trumps interconnect the formula of the Triune Goddess ~ of Maiden-Mother-Crone averse, or rather, Virgin-Whore-Crone.

Artemis-Maria Immaculata-Cybele-Isis is the Eternal Virgin, the Black Madonna clothed in the luminous veil of the Stars. Initiation into the mysteries of Isis lead the candidate to that Light is not the perfect manifestation of the Eternal Spirit; She is the supernal light that veils matter and form. She is the luminous idea of spirit acting through matter, descending through the Abyss to annul the space between generation and sexual instinct.

Alma Māter consoles and protects, yet she also punishes and condemns. Mary Beth Moser in her book Honoring Darkness: Exploring the Power of Black Madonnas in Italy {see Bibliography} dedicates a whole section to the Madonna's "Punishing Miracles" {pp. 68-76}. Her divine acts of justice avert the desecration of Her countenance and ensure earthly respect for the Alma Māter. Alma Māter is not heiress to the thrones of all the matrilineal goddesses, if She is limited to one sexual nature or one color. Black Madonna guards the lost, derelict, and those maddened with love and lust, She not only births the incarnation of the Sun to us, but also guards the secrets of death. Hence one of Her Catholic titles: Our Lady of the Good Death.

The Black Madonna's link to death is evidenced by the title of the Black Virgin of Clermont-Ferrand, and that many of her icons were venerated in subterranean burial chapels {crypts} of the great medieval Cathedrals. Consider Our Lady from Under the Ground {Notre Dame de Sous Terre}, the Black Madonna in the crypt of Cathedral Chartres, whose poetic title "Our Lady of the Underworld" is befitting of her custodianship over the spirit at the moment of death. Catholics venerate the Black Madonna profoundly, as a custodian and guide after death. Her prayer, the Ave Maria, ends thusly: "pray for us sinners, now and at the hour of our death." This is a mantra repeated over and over when praying with her rosary.

Convents, statues, cathedrals, even confraternities are named after Our Lady of the Good Death, ever placing a mantle of mystery and adoration upon the Black Madonna. In 19th century Brazil a Confraternity of Our Lady of the Good Death, made up of African slaves, was instrumental in synthesizing African and Catholic traditions into what came to be known as 'Candomble,' and 'Santeria.' To this day, there exists a Confraternity of "Catholic" Women of Our Lady of the Good Death in Cachoeira, Brazil, who are responsible for the survival of indigenous folklore in the form of Candomble and Santeria.

Black Madonna icons often measure 70 centimeters in height, 30 cm in width, and 30 cm in depth. The 7:3 ratio echoes sacred numerology that goes back to pre-Christian history. In the Christian context, the 7:3 speaks of Trinitarianism {the 3 mystic complements of the trinity} and the seven mystic days for Genesis, the creations of the known archetypal worlds. Black Madonnas were enshrined at places that were sacred even before Christianity, pagan holy sites and natural vortices of biorhythmic energies.

Legend recounts that Saint Eusebius {martyred 371 A.D.}, led by divine inspiration, found the Our Lady of Oropa icon in Jerusalem, buried under ancient ruins. Eusebius brought her to Italy and enthroned her in a grotto sacred to Ceres, Roman goddess of the earth, in order to end the local pagan rituals. The woods around it were consecrated to Apollo and the large rocks to Ceres and Diana. Our Lady of Oropa became quite attached to this grotto. A group of Benedictine monks tried to move the icon to a new location a thousand years after Eusebius' relocation of it. Yet after ew miles, the statue grew too heavy for the monks to transport, and they had to return it to the grotto.

Shrines to the Black Madonna all have a connection with the Benedictines, the Cistercians, or the Knights Templars. All three of these orders were strongly influenced by Saint Bernard {1090- 1153}, who was instrumental in establishing a pervasive and fervent popular cult of the Virgin. Vatican scholars list less than 50 of early 'pagan' Black Madonnas whose faces and hands are often painted a dark brown or black pigmentation. American scholars at the University of Dayton, Ohio report at least 450 Black Madonna icons in Belgium, Brazil, Croatia, Ecuador, England, France, Germany, Hungary, Ireland, Italy, Lithuania, Luxemburg, Malta, Mexico, Poland, Portugal, Romania, Spain, and Switzerland.

In the Jungian school of psychology, the Black Madonna represents the archetype of the dark feminine: the unexplored, unpredictable, and unexperienced in humans and in the Godhead. She represents the existential terror one succumbs to in the St. John of the Cross' "dark night of the soul" in order to achieve gnosis. Cedrus N. Monte calls the Black Madonna a "lethal force" to Man's ego. Monte explains that when the ego is lethally wounded, the true self experiences the crisis of rebirth, a form of transient death often experienced in ceremonial initiations.

The Black Madonna, Isis the Black Virgin, represents a continuity of life, a heritage of blood that binds nature and Man together. There is no breach between space and dark matter; the ancients worshipped the Great Goddess of the Earth as the primordial Alma Māter who nourishes all Life. The virginal Alma Māter is the perfection of Nature, birthing the Christ-Horus Child which takes the place of the Son {Vau} acting through the Father {Yod} in the formula of the Tetragrammaton.

Concealed in the very Mystical Memory of Woman and of the Genetrix, is the beginnings of the pagan agrarian period with its fertility rites and matriarchal adorations; the worship of Isis, the Holy Mother proceeded by the Christian Age with patriarchal worship of Man and solar-phallic worship with the religious legends of the Dying God Slain and Risen; this in turn is consummated by the contemporary Æon of the Childe, the Two-In- One as an antinomian undercurrent whereby is enthroned the Crowned and Conquering Childe who avenges in Lust and imperial Love allayed by carnal sorrows and uninhibited eroticism.

The old æon of Pisces enshrouded the human species into spiritual bondage, as all cognate religious of the old æon adore Death, glorify suffering, and deify corpses in the images of the abominable crucifix and its implications. By the destruction of the esoteric principle of Death an antinomian undercurrent of the Lilith prototype births that breaks down all psychosexual ideologies and matrices initiated by previous eons.

The hyper-feminist attitudes prevailing in Western Societies {refer yourselves to the enlightened research of Wilhelm Reich, Julius Evola, Carl Gustav Jung, Sigmund Freud, Barbara Black Koltuv who warned us about sexual feminism} indicates a return to a degenerate Judaic understanding of sex. Each era and procession of the zodiacal æon begins a more de-evolved form of human sexuality and eroticism in religious motifs, with new psychotechnology as the brain adapts to new interpretations of cultural and religious memes.

The function of initiates into the mysteries of the Black Madonna is to restore balance to the spiritual and natural roles of women. The racial blood memories of the Sangréal infers a rebirth from the ashes of severe trauma {initiation}. The witches, nuns, Gurus and Gurujis, Bishops, Deacons, warlocks, and Magi whom have pasted the tests of evolution and reached into the depths of their primacy inherit the royal blood. The sanga-lugal was the priest-king in ancient Sumer, from whence comes the French Sangréal, the 'blood royal.' The legendary Holy Grail, popularly ascribed to be the metaphysical womb of the Magdalene, existed contextually long before Jesus Christ.

In context of antiquated rites of mystical marriage, the *hierodule* {Greek, hierodulous} served as a female acolyte, often in connotation with religious prostitution. This sacred prostitute referred to as the Scarlet Woman, allegorized as the Whore of Babylon in Revelations, was the holy aspect of ancient bridal rituals of the orient. Her sacred hieroglyph was the Rosi-Crucis, a cross within a circle found in many ancient religious sites and Roman coinage.

The ceremonial robes of the *heirodulai*, the sacred prostitutes were scarlet red, and in lieu of the Madonna's sacerdotal role, many medieval artists such as Luca Signorelli and Caravaggio portray Mary in red garments. The Song of Inanna reciprocated by the New Testament Song of Solomon indicates an antiquated ritual of mystical marriage. The Christ and Magdalene epitomize the Hieros Gamos, a mystical marriage that often reconciles and obscures the borders between sexuality and religion.

Isis is the dance of Life itself. She is constantly sashaying and writhing in ecstasy, as all the primal possibilities of Nature and sex are enjoyed under the phantom shadow of space and matter. All of Nature and the procession of the eons are harmony and beauty to the Black Virgin; her sacred words are perfect love and perfect trust. The Black Madonna is always depicted swathed in the shawl of secrecy, vaporous because she is occult; She is the sphinx whom delegates the Secret yet is without secrets. she is the Graal, the container of the ethereal waters, which are blood, oil, sperm, and menses. Often associated with Isis is Venus, represented by the obtuse and acute Heptagram.

The Black Madonna is the vaporous guardian over the threshold of life and death, "Our Lady of the Good Death," recall is the Goddess many Christians invoke upon death and is often invoked in the Last Rites. She is all mysterious, all nourishing, all enticing, all intoxicating, ever immaculate, and diaphanous.

Recall that, as Isis the Black Madonna is the nourishing Alma Māter, she also is the Lady of Sorrows for she is the Alma Māter and Nature is Her name. As the trumpets of the zodiacal processions and their mythic apocalypses blare forth the fearful glories of Isis, at the end is the deathly silence of the Black Madonna.

Black Madonnas

Onze-Lieve-Vrouw van Regula Moeder van Regula van Spaignen Brugge Chapelle de la Vierge Noire, Maillen Assesse, Belgium Donji Kraljevec, County of Medjimurje, Croatia Our Lady of Rocamadour Saint Saveur d'Aix, Aix-en-Provence Avioth, Meuse, France Our Lady of Altötting, Bavaria, Germany
Our Lady of Dublin, Ireland

Our Lady of Tindari, Sicily, Italia

Black Madonna of Oropa, Piedmont, Italia

Our Lady of Crea, Casale Monferrato, Alessandria Il-Madonna tas-Samra Madonna of Samaria, Malta The Black Madonna of Częstochowa, Poland Theotokos of St. Theodore, Russia
Our Lady Of Atocha, Madrid, Spain

The Virgin in the Monastery of Santa María de Guadalupe Virgin of Montserrat in Catalonia, Spain

Nuestra Señora de la Merced {Our Lady Of Mercy}, Jerez de la Frontera, Cádiz, Spain

The Virgin of the Miracles, Virgen de los milagros, El Puerto de Santa María, Cádiz, Spain

Our Lady of the Hermits, Einsiedeln, Switzerland

Santa Maria Loretana, Sonogno, Valle Verzasca, Switzerland Black Madonnas or important replicas in the Americas

Our Lady of Aparecida, Brazil La Negrita, Cartago, Costa Rica Black Madonna Shrine, Missouri, United States

National Shrine of Our Lady of Czestochowa, Pennsylvania, United States

VI

Ad cubavit lamia
(A post-addendum to the Rite of Lilith)

Nigredo burns. Its tutelary signs, cold wind, deep echoes, are there when we delve into the dimension beyond. It is beyond every nation and state, beyond every border, beyond the polluted roots of nature, beyond the paths of communication, beyond every voice of reason that says to wake up to life. The Nihil lies beyond, and we are very naive if we ignore it.

Ironically, only through great inner strife and disbelief to every reason will one arrive there. The bastions of reason and order tell us to worship life, the declining patriarchal order, and its rotten structures. While turning the tide, reversing his or her laws, we find what lies beyond and is feared by everyone: the Infinite, the Nothing. Is this what they have been fighting against since His name was erased from the temples many thousands of years ago?
The New Flesh of the Axis...we that stand against the regime and declare annihilation of the structures...actually has to be a corpus of multipartite matrix burning feverously in knowledge. Beyond darkness:

Alma Māter glimpsed in the perfect black, inside the infinite, stillness among the spheres and the flux of Might that is directed to the hearts of those who know. Drinking from the holiest mysteries, iconoclasts like the Catholics reveal Her as matrix of Divinity, Bearer of Life without external intervention, all-powerful, autonomous, a deity, carrying both unity of matter and duality/ability to fracture.

Indeed, the majority recognizes Thee Source as a mere, bland, passive emblem of Jew submission to chastity, motherhood, and obedience, the eternally cursed matrices of LYLYT, clearly dismissing her infinite Might. The candid white figure that millions worship daily representing the ever submissive and pitiful mother of God is no other than the hidden Might, Eternal Sea of Darkness, Infinite Nothing, Death and Chaos, in whose name is all power given {L.A.V.L. I;15}.

As the processes of new age spirituality, the Age of Aquarius, the frenzy of free love and the gaiety of Wicca along with the cheerful Gardnerian covens not only helped to build bland, innocuous "holy mother" worship, also produced a fundamental mutation, which was the socially acceptable detour from Judaism, still disillusioned on the equality myth.

Such softcore pagan matrilineal allowed a sensible rebuilding of the structures and mystical paths that had been oppressed since the fall of the Elden Gods as, with their athame and handfastings and Lady and Lord, waged a silent war against the instituted Semitic curses. Nevertheless, everything turns into smut, since their own structures are shallow and dissipative, for they do not allow the so-called dark side to emerge.

What lies hidden, beyond, and is feared by all: there is nothing to fear when one looks into the eyes of the abyss. To leave everything behind and plunge into the inky blackness that awaits, to free one's heart from mortal fears: seems so difficult yet it is the Key to Eternity, to transcend the mere human dimension. They, with the threefold laws and banishing, fear and avoid the element that inexorably traps them all.

When merging the Nothing, everything becomes a warped system, a still structure, manifesting the echo of what is continuous and infinite; it is nowhere, and everywhere to be found: inside. One's journey into the Nothing, where the Black Sun lies beyond everything, can be severely traumatic: Love breaches the nexus between lust, desire, flesh, and everywhere in these dimensions. We who let the mighty victories of our Gods perish those who mock the stories of their ethereal flesh only rejoice with each soul's maddening dive into the perils of love.

Love is Not...so where will you rest in the final dimensions of bliss? A few pathetic vags under the flag of neo-paganism still insist about worshipping life, based on Jewish Kabbalist cults and vagina-centered spirituality: all for Man, a warrior's reward, and earthen garbage disposal. They see the infinite Curses of Lilith as Cause to the Void, where Everything and Nothing resumes to NOT...absolute Nihil, Nigredo...the horrible Black.

NOT means Death, as death cults are concerned with the worship and lust for death...death according to a ritual "game." It is alchemical process in full flux, which to all beliefs, myths, and legends still bows down in karmic debt. Ironically, Lilith worshipped as the primeval source of lust and life, also is the Source of the End...of Death itself.

As Man falls into the crystalline sea of the Abyss, a death leap into the well of pain, one finds the earthen mysteries of life and death pointless. Dimensions fade, borders melt, oceans part, and gods die...an infinite plain between existence and the end, lying at the very origin of Lilith's curse. It is yet a frightening world for those who seek it not, for those who know it not...as the human species finds itself deep into Nihil, naked, unarmed, leaving absolutely everything ...life ... beliefs...protections abandoned, torn asunder from the racial and psychological comfort, for in the meaning of life Lilith either loses Her mind from sheer terror or finds Her True Nature, becomes one with N.O.T., fused into the Void, becoming Cause, human dimension dissolved with no trace of existence left.

Mithraic cults adapted with almost no modification the ritual disembowelment of a bull that was done previously unto Cybele, certainly an outrageous figure to emergent patriarchal Neophytes, to whom an almighty Goddess whose priests emasculated themselves gleefully to adore Her in blood, and to whose honor monks and initiates engaged in wild frenzied sex orgies were thrown, conducted by Sacred Prostitutes, was a threat, an unending terror...Lilith's curse uncovered, as Judaic priests with impotent dicks can only revel in homosexuality and gather to rip off immemorial traditions.

In Mesopotamian motifs, the *Enuma Elish*, the slaying of *Tiamat*, ancient goddess of the primal underworld and chaos, happens from the *Marduk's* hand. Marduk emasculates Tiamat and scatters her body through the firmament rearranging constellations and spaces between the stars. "Above, the gemmed azure is/The naked splendor of Nuit" {L.A.V.L. I;14}. Since I am Infinite Space, and the Infinite Stars thereof {L.A.V.L. I;22} accentuates this legend. After the Master of Babylon declares himself King, he is the impersonation of Patriarchy, organized pyramidal hierarchic structures, improvised laws, and established religions.

Thus, Lilith can only reflect and never guide Mankind to what existed before All, beyond All, transcending all...Infinite Nihil, Infinite Abyss, Infinite Void, Infinite Xaos. The entity present in each and every religious tradition...the Beast, the Serpent, the infernal depths, Death, beyond all that, the Nothing...the inexplicable, eternal darkness and silence...the secret of Her magical formula is Nothing = Nothing, 0 = 0. Even the Christian Genesis agrees with this formula, as the Bible states God wrought creatio ex nihilo. Everywhere, collapsing dimensions screaming Magna Māter in the background, which is the same Not...the Void that unfolds thee Eternal.

All hidden, secret Cause wrought by Her...Death, Void, Not, Chaos, the Axis {Arabic, *Qutub*} is still labeled as the patrilineal caveat of religion. The cursed by Lilith, walk naked, lewd, and lecherous, at Her constant mercy across the abyss, the black path consists in enabling the Core of the Semitic Structure, welcoming in body and mind the rejection of the solar Aryan enlightenment, feeling in our souls the Transcendental Tempest and the Spiritual Fury.

Lilith's black magicians declare war to every established religion and cult. We despise peaceful, even fakery perfumed in occultism, thelemic associations, who do nothing but hold in their hands sacred, precious knowledge unable and unwilling to decode without the help of the Black Sun!

They Torch the mosques of Mecca and unveil the Lady of the Black Shawl in all Her nakedness! Raid the Vatican and dig under the cathedrals of Europa for the Truth to be Known! Burn Crowley's Libri and emasculate the Beast upon the thorns of His Christ! Possess, and be possessed. Explore the edges of sanity and descend into primacy. The awe, the joy, the emotions and the magic released are beyond description, and the undercurrents infinite.

Each word, kiss, act, are holy deeds in the divine joy of nature. The violence of nature's desire. Primal. Chthonian. Joined in the bonds of perfect Lust, the greatest joy is to give joy. Giving and receiving of joy is a blessing in its own, a sacrament and a long, slow, effective prayer. The ecstasy it reaches, the deepness of the abyss of NOT that both have become, the pleasure, the ecstasy shared is deeper than the deepest abyss. Lust, unleashed. Primal, intense, violent, magical.

The Semitic racialist curse confirms LYLYT as evil, forbidden, irrelevant. It is a rejection to the established White Gods. Because it knows it cannot escape from it, that eventually it will be mercilessly engulfed back again to the dregs of ignominy where it should have never had emerged. Kali dances upon the Shiva's wielding death in Her eight hands. Tiamat's children are venomous snakes, enraged hounds, minotaurs, and centaurs.

The One that calls in the Desert, the deep of the Abyss, the Negra Deam of the Axis is the Chthonian Black Madonna; source of racialist hatred, hatred of Mankind, and diablerie. Meanwhile Lilith's Semitic scum under the flag of prophecy and "magick" dwell in holy places, blithering about old lore, despising what truly lies within flesh. Instead of realizing the perfection of the White Gods, of the One True God, they thrive in the habit of denying it to some improvised archetypes and corruptions of Law.

The Semitic black magicians of Lilith see Oppression itself as liberation. Black Mother enables diseases of blood and mind facing this emerging of lies. Their children are the People of the Lie. This liberal or progressive culture, endowed with a toxic elitism, is the enemy for every Knower, whose stand does not bow, does not make any concessions as His heart is consumed. I will make my enemy defend me. If I have any friend here let him turn away his eyes. Lilith is a dead Goddess, a cursed rejection of Light.

Lilith has Her form repeated in motifs across various cultures, and the blackness is behind them all. The Law is one, in the core of NOT. Law is trinity and three is one, not dead and revealed or alive and alight, but benighted and hidden. in the center of the earth: in the heart of the burned fields. I remain. I come as a mighty warrior and for the holy princess to be crowned without knowing such as the one from Her Radix was once crowned. Virgo de stirps Matrem/Imperator de radice Matrem. Seek a lake that does not know its own thirst, the safe Northern mountain, the river without blood and water, the fields where nothing remains but the voices, the forest of love entwined, the night wailing without end. In the desert, seven souls shall curse me.

Blood shall spill from our holy conquests, washing away the radix and the lands of the cursed Semites and their black Gods, cascading down into a new vine for our sons to harvest. You shall find me there, I will speak to you in your mind's core...I shall ascend from the holy soils of Europa to open your eyes. You shall bleed. You will cry. Our blood and soil is sacred to me. Revelation is heavy in might and true in spirit for those who seek it. Now go and do your task, but never lose way from your Path...brave men, do not lose breath, the mighty warrior shall not fall. Kings will rise and fall, but in the end the cunning shall stand. Be brave and seek the truth in the pools of Aryan eyes.

VII

The Black Kabbalah

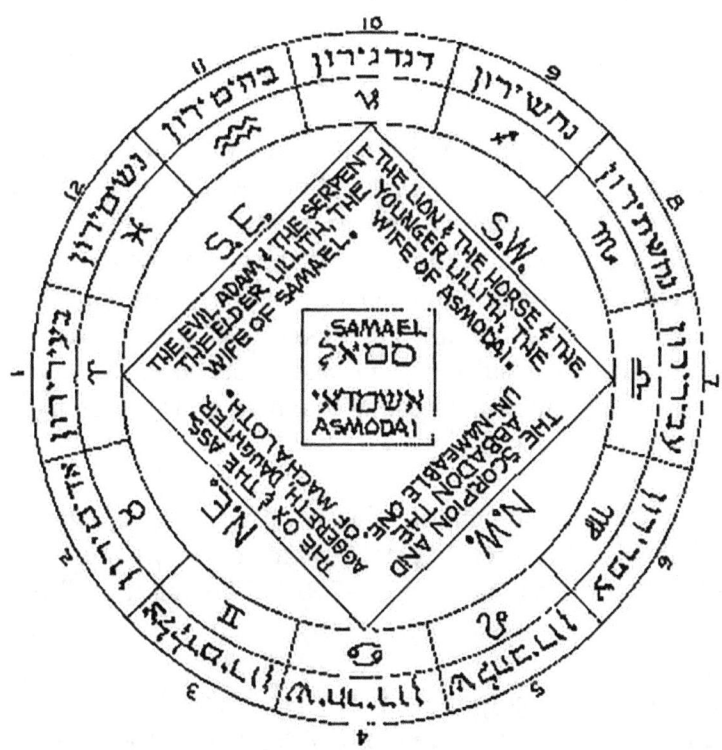

God and our known universe mediate between ten principles called Sefirot, the fundamentals of existence. Since the universe is in perfect chaotic symmetry, the principles of evil and the 'Klippoth,' should be distinguished in human moral evil. Evil in a Hermetic sense is that which is entropic, has no being, the thing that appears to be but is not, that leads to separation of the divine light and providence. When the immaterial fluidic venom of the entered into man, it

poisoned him and all nature, which then became susceptible to evil's influence. Human nature was darkened and made into coarse matter, as man received a corporeal body, a shard or husk – a Kelippot; at the same time the whole 'Asiyyatic world, of which man had been the lord and master, was condensed and coarsened in shells of divine light.

The twenty-two Hebrew letters are a boundary-line, demarcating the spiritual and physical world (Malchut), constituting the form of matter cognizable by language – the human capacity for thought-organization. It is in language and the conceiving of thought that evil is given form. Klippoth, kliffoth, or klippot, is derived from the Hebrew term qelippot, meaning "peels", "shells" or "husks".

The Klippoth in Kabbalah are antithetical to the seppirot. Klippoth are the ten {eleven, counting the Kliphah of Da'ath} manifestations of demonic, or entropic forces, into which God's divine light cannot reach. The Klippoth are the personifications of an "anti-God" condition, or demonic personifications of entropy. Hasidic theology proposes that in the process of creation, ten seppirot were created, each encapsuled by a kliphah, a peel of creation that contains the secrets of matter manifesting into both divine light and entropic personified darkness.

The earliest mention of a Tree of Life in the Scriptures is in Genesis 3:22 (Masoretic Text). The date of the writing of this text by the Yahwist Priesthood was 750-700^{BC}. The Semitic tribes held 'sacred tree' symbolism prominently in their religious beliefs. The Sumerians were the first to depict a Sacred Tree; a Tree of Life. Babylon priests incorporated it in their mythos from the Sumerians when they overthrew their empire. Assyria then took it from the Babylonians in turn when they conquered the Babylonian empire, as the chain of Tree of Life symbolism continued into the medieval interpretations of the Kabbalah. Culturally speaking, the Tree of Life is Sumerian in origin.

According to Helena P. Blavatsky, the Jews acquired their Kabbalistic cosmology from the Chaldeans, later developing into a writing compendium of theurgy, cosmology, and mysticism: *"Kabbalah (Heb.) The hidden wisdom of the Hebrew Rabbis of the middle ages derived from the older secret doctrines concerning divine*

things and cosmogony, which were combined into a theology after the time of the captivity of the Jews in Babylon. All the works that fall under the esoteric category are termed Kabalistic." (Blavatsky, Theosophical Glossary, p. 168) The Pythagorean idea of the creative powers of numbers and letters, upon which the Sefer Yetzirah corroborates deep in the Tannaitic era, proves to be an old cabalistic representations.

The belief in the magic power of the letters of the Tetragrammaton originates in Chaldea (Lenormant, 'Chaldean Magic,' pp. 29, 43). Since Abraham, and not a Talmudic hero like Akiba, is introduced in the 'Sefer Yetzirah,' as possessor of the Wisdom of the Alphabet and Letters, indicates an old tradition of esoteric transmission. The dualistic cosmology of good and of evil powers derives from Zoroastrianism and ultimately old Chaldea, influencing the cosmology of the ancient Kabbalah before it reached the medieval Kabbalistic literature. The gradual condensation of primeval substance into visible matter, a fundamental Kabbalistic doctrine, creatio ex nihilo, is the ancient Semitic conception of the primal ocean of the unfathomable Abyss, known to the Babylonians as Apsu.

In the medieval Jewish Kabbalistic literature, old ideas from Babylon gained new strength. The *Klippoth*, or *Kelippot* (קליפות the primeval "peels" of impurity), was blamed for all the evil in the world. The *Klippoth* are found in the old Babylonian incantations, a fact used as evidence in favor of the antiquity of most of the cabalistic material."

Evidence indicates that Kabbalistic theurgy derives from ancient Mesopotamian sources and was demonized since 'foreign deities' could not fit into the Jewish pantheon. Moreover, the term *klippot*, meaning peel, or 'husk,' did not initially describe "evil" in its inception. It is interesting to note that the combination sign for 'peel' corresponds with a pregnant woman, also; a body with water in it. The Sumerian word is *iskilla*; the Akkadian *isqillatu*.

The Babylonians worshipped a Goddess Mother and a Son, who was represented secret doctrines concerning divine things and cosmogony, which were combined into a theology after the time of the captivity of the Jews in Babylon. All the works that fall under the esoteric category are termed Kabalistic." (Blavatsky, Theosophical

Glossary, p. 168) The Pythagorean idea of the creative powers of numbers and letters, upon which the Sefer Yetzirah refers to the Tannaitic era, proving again old Kabbalistic representations. The belief in the magic power of the letters of the Tetragrammaton originates in Chaldea (Lenormant, 'Chaldean Magic,' pp. 29, 43). Since Abraham, and not a Talmudic hero like Akiba, is introduced in the 'Sefer Yetzirah,' as possessor of the Wisdom of the Alphabet and Letters, indicates an old tradition of esoteric transmission.

The Klippoth are the antithetical principle behind theurgy, and religious philosophy; it represents the personification of entropy. The symmetry of Light in the Kabbalah represents geometric and mathematical principles in which God manifested the universe. The Klippoth represent fractals and divisive forces, though if harnessed properly in the human mind can wield unnatural means of enlightenment. The use of Klippotic principles in magic can free the adept from the limits of cultural myth and conceptual archetypes of creation.

This path sometimes is referred to as "Luciferian," and "Typhonian" magic, yet I prefer the more archaic Draconian. The Klippoth opens primeval transphysical gates, or as Frater Kenneth Grant referred to them, "tunnels," the Unknown Lands that no religious map has ever charted. Adepts who lived in the deserts and the wastelands and spoken with demons and the souls of slaughtered men, and of women who have died in childbirth, obsessions, and creatures which rupture the fabric of human consciousness, all would likely attest to Klippotic experiences.

Klippotic powers are found in the buried psychological grottos of the human mind in the form of obsessions, fetishes, and undeveloped personalities; beneath the monuments of vanquished civilizations millennia olde, between the black infinities of outer space where science and religion disappear in a nexus of uncertainty. Assuming brazenly that Klippotic powers are primeval, predating Judeo-Christian theology, one can command and beseech the Unshaped Demons of the Dead Worlds to indwell within. Great care must be taken in Klippotic meditations and conjurations as these powers are primeval and can rapidly possess the mind and "spirit" of a human being, leading to swift or gradual self-destruction and horrific insanity.

Alternatively, if an Adept uses Klippotic magic in a more experiential manner; without external Spirits or (Arch) Demons, one can invoke the principles of the Klippoth from deep within the wells of human psyche, or as Carl G. Jung called it, the "Shadow." Great care must be taken again when invoking Klippotic forces as part of your psyche which can just as easily imbalance the mind and cause permanent psychological damage. Such damage to the subconscious and waking mind could theoretically destroy the functioning personality, with the magician unaware in a state of psychic shock; believing one's "self" to be perfectly of 'sound mind.'

I recommend one's ideological principles to be established and clear while working with the Klippoth. A college level understanding of psychology and a few fields such as abnormal, behavioral, humanistic, criminal should be studied some time before actual Klippotic work begins, and also concurrently. It is dire for the magician to understand that the Klippotic principles mirror primeval forces, some of which lay dormant in the majority of the human brain, save for a small collection of artists, composers, criminals, national world leaders, and other mutated draconian brains imprisoned within human flesh. If a magician has self-destructive tendencies then self-destruction will undoubtedly result in Klippotic working. I personally know of two "magicians" encapsulated in a life spanning creeping insanity.

Samuel Liddell MacGregor Mathers puts his Judaic Masonic prejudice full on display in his lectures Philosophi of the old Hermetic Golden Dawn on the Klippoth. Macgregor's interpretation of the Klippoth is a near miss, stricken with Jewish-instilled curse of 'perverted spheres.' "These be they who are Unclean and Evil, even the Distortion and Perversion of the Sefiroth; the fallen restriction of the Universe; the rays of the Coils of the Stooping Dragon. Eleven are their classes, yet Ten are they called; seven are the heads and yet an eighth head arises.

Seven are the Infernal Palaces, yet do they include Ten. In the Tree of Life, by the Waters of the River, in the Garden of Wisdom, is the serpent of the Paths; it is the Serpent of the Celestial

Eden. But the Serpent of the Temptation is that of the Tree of Knowledge of Good and Evil; the antithesis and opposer of the other: the Red Coiled Stooping Dragon of the Apocalypse, the Serpent of the Terrestrial Eden."

The demonization of life is one of the most effective and dangerous factors in the development of the Kabbalah. The dangers of magic influencing the religious and pious minds of early Judaism are exemplified in the development of the Kabbalah. Early Kabbalistic philosophers such as Isaac Luria believed the Klippoth to be also a scene of the soul's exile, of a demonization of the world of nature and human existence. Lurianic Kabbalism refers to the Klippoth as the demonic "Other Side," the sitra ahra. The accursed racialist black magicians of Lilith study the Klippoth as a cultural meme, and transformational force in practices of magic and sociology.

The cortices, and the first races developed their praeter- human powers from the Chthonian magic that originated with and from the earth, not from hybrid ancestral human "spirits" and Jewish ancestral magic. Predating Isaac Luria's system and his teachings of partzufim, or "independent spiritual manifestations" (see Simon bar Yochai in the Zohar), Klippoth were described in Neo-Platonist theory as demonic entities from a former universe whose "husks" and cortices remain in the present one.

These shells came from a primeval anomaly, sentient agencies of chaos and entropy {the remnants spuriously mentioned in texts such as the Necronomicon, Grimoire of Honorius, and Bundahishn} that were obfuscated during early stages of the creation of the cosmos, theoretically perhaps when "God" attempted to "Know Itself" via prima causa, the First Cause.

Luria describes the Sefir Sefirot as orderly creation interrupted by disaster, thereby putting limitations on the omnipotence of YHVH. The agents that were meant to retain the seven Sefirot from Chesed to Malchut were inadequate, breached in the face of the descending current of creative light, the "Stooping Serpent." The Klippoth emerged from the shards of the dead universes, reanimated by cortices of divine light still retained within. The use of demonic, or Klippotic, powers greatly attract the human brain, seeking unfathomable explanations of its transphysical origin and purpose.

As the human species began to master magic, the species sank into the Klippot, the reflection of the world of Assiah upon the chaos of human passions, leading to the mythic creation of Hell - the materialized fathomless mental pit. The human condition has not yet fulfilled nor unveiled any limit. It is an ongoing progression toward omneity, identity and innate divinity, or what Initiates testify to as the Mystery. Throughout the spiritual epoch of the human species, evil is self-evident as a misperceived illusion which excels religious premise and theological perspective.

A historical exegesis of the Devil as phenomenalized evil must be countered with abstractivity and mythology. Jung's analysis of the Devil as archetypal schism of the psyche reflect the Rabbinic teaching that two antagonistic essences inhabit the nefesch; one a tendency to preconceived righteousness (yetser ha'tob) and the other a tendency to 'evil' (yetser ha'ra).

The Devil defuses metaphysically into allegory of evil inclinations, Ancient Egyptian theology is polytheistic, alive with anthropomorphism, animism, and deification. Osirian religion in ancient Egypt fashioned notions of evil designed from empyrean conflict seen in the lore of the slaying and resurrection of Ausar. There is no implicit principle of evil in such monographs as the 'Pyramid Texts,' the "Papyrus of Nebseni,' or vignettes from the 'Papyrus of Ani.' In ancient Egyptian theology, evil is the maleficious disruption of Ma'at.

Antagonism between Sutekh (SUTI) and Heru (HOORI) incarnates the dread of death and ignorance of natural Law in the human condition. Suti originally was a deity native to institutions in Hyksos, presiding over desert winds and the arts of combat. The politically antagonistic relationship between Heru and Sutekh retains an erotic venture with reference to Sutekh's incestuous rape of Heru in the 'Pyramid Texts.'

Subsequent to Hyksos 'incursions,' initiates dwelling along a fertile landscape whose bloodline was the Nile dreaded the withering heat of the Sun in the South, which brought agrarian sterility and ruin. Suti derives from sût, "red" akin to the colored hue of the desert, the bodily figure of Suti shapes an image of a mortal with the head of an unidentified mythological animal called the "sut animal,' akin to an ass or jackal. As late as the XXIInd Dynasty, Sutekh was besought for reinforcement and sanction in the arts of warfare.

The deity Sutekh (Setekh, Sut) is unrecognizable as any animal at present. Set was identified also with the hippopotamus, the pig, and ass, often abhorred by Egyptians along the fertile banks of the Nile river. Such beasts were sacred to the god of winds, as well as crocodiles, scorpions, turtles, and other contentious beasts thought to devour the phallus of Osiris after Set dismembered Him. The 'sût' animal was postulated to possess long jackal-like squared ears, a long stooping snout, and a canine-like body. Such could possibly be a composite beast part aardvark, part canine or even camel.

The cult of Heru (HOORI) likely overtook SUTI following Hyksos insurgency during the Second Intermediate Period, as Sût ceased to symbolize Lower Egypt. During the Third Intermediate Period Sutekh became associated with foreign insurgency, thus transfiguring his divinity to chaos and warfare. To the Ægyptians of the lower Nile region, he was the god who 'ate the moon each month,' the 'black boar who swallowed Khonsu.'

In the Hebrew Torah and in the Talmud, inclusive of mainstream Judaic tradition, the Devil is never distinguished as a Chthonic ruler of an 'evil empire' of diabolical Hosts. The Satan appears first in Numbers, Job, and Zechariah as prosecutor for the Heavenly Court, not as a Fallen rebellious with designs against Yahweh or humans. Etymology of the 'satan' stems from the Hebrew root, śṭn, a verb meaning 'to obstruct.' A few Rabbinic theologians, refuted naturally, pose śṭn (śāṭān) to be derived also from the Hebrew root, šūt, "to rove about." Thus, we have also the Greek term, 'diabolos,' literally 'to obstruct something.'

The Satan of the Torah was thus a roving hierarchical prosecutor, obstructing human infallibility. The Arabic derivative šaiṭān and the substantive śṭnā, also the Arabic root sh'y'ṭ, does not appear in the Noble Qu'ran as a designation of evil. In the Book of Job, the Satan is an inculpator, implicating humanity in false predilections of Yahweh. In the Book of Zechariah, the Satan is a divine Host of retribution, inciting factional division and warfare within the tribes of Israel.

The mal'āk Yahweh of the Book of Numbers obstructs the Balaam, the human as an adversary. It is in this appearance, Numbers 22:22 do we glance upon the ambivalent resistance of the divine to Mankind. Only in I Chronicles XXI; v.1 and II Samuel XXIV; v.1 the term śāṭān is used as a proper noun. The intimacy of these passages refers to a defined personality, as contrasting indefiniteness would leave theological ambiguity.

The passages in the Book of Numbers as well as Zechariah pose the concept of the Satan opposing Mankind inimically as an independent personification of evil. At the time of the Maccabean War, splinter-sectarian movements such as the aesthetic Essences bolstered eschatology as the political and religious thrust of their austere and secretive Brotherhood. Metaphysical war reflected the Maccabean revolt and desire of the Brethren for a New Israel in the "Scroll of the War of the Sons of Light against the Sons of Darkness." Had the Satan not existed in the Torah, the Essenes calling themselves the 'Sons of Light' would have invented Him.

Bishop of Lyons, Irenaeus (140-202 CE) rejected the Gnostic sectarians in favor of Pauline orthodoxy. Bishop Irenaeus was foremost preoccupied with defending the Pauline Church against early internal dissent. The tracts of Irenaeus echo those of his later contemporary, Bishop Tertullian (170-220 CE) of Carthage. The Satan apostatized in their Justinian philosophy and was now presented in the Church as an eminent metaphysical potency.

The Christology of Irenaeus and Tertullian professed the crucifixion as a recapitulation, undoing original sin. The providence of the Satan was granted solely from Mankind's misuse of Will, as the Willed sacrifice canceled out the rights of the Satan. The Satan was approved a Luciferian quality as atonement became for Theologians, synonymous with sacrifice. God and the Devil were redefined by Irenaeus and Tertullian as antimony of ethical opposites. Saeculum

(the cosmos) and saecularia (the material) reflected the ideal of evil as created, not an independent principle.
Saint Augustine of Hippo (354-430 A.D.) abandons a Manichean influence he once early espoused in the question of Theodicy.

Augustine's literary approach, in such works as the "City of God" and "Confessions" returns Us to the ideal of evil lacking intrinsic substance. Augustine writes in his Retractionum Libri Duo (421 A.D): "*Malvm non exortvm nisi ex libero voluntatis arbitrio*" (evil does not arise except through free choice of Will). In his Confessiones (397 A.D), he writes: "*Nemo igitur qua erat efficientem causam malae volvntatis; non enim est efficiens sed deficiens, quia nec illa effectio sed defectio.*" ('no man must ask the efficient cause of an evil Will, for the cause is deficient, not efficient; an evil will is a defect').

Augustine saw the principle of evil as ontological privation Evil, according to his work "De libero arbitrio" (385-3954 A.D), is ascribed to sin as an ontological defect, an insurgency of the Will upon Itself as both preordained and fallible. Saint Augustine attributes evil to a defective movement of Will, by choice, averse to predestination. Wrote Augustine: "*Mali enim nulla natura est; sed amisso boni mali nomen accepit*" ('evil has no nature; what is named evil is a lack of good'). The latter from the "City of God" (421 A.D) illustrates the heart of evil as privation, contrary to a personified ideal.

The views of Saint Augustine are grounded in traditional Christian theodicy. Later Christian Theologians such as Thomas Aquinas (1225-1274 A.D), and Saint Anselm (1033-1109 A.D) perpetuated the debate of evil as an ontological principle, of an embodiment of sin in Mankind. Saint Anselm and Thomas Aquinas were the foremost theologians whom initiated an advent of Scholasticism, and its three pillars of Christian Theology.
Scripture, orthopraxy, and analysis of scriptural tradition are the pillars of the Christian scholastic movement. The role of the Satan in theology declined with the advent of Its metaphysical presence in History.

The immediacy of the Luciferian Devil reduced the archetype to a theological novelty. Saint Anselm's ambivalent answer to scholastic theodicy was that evil is nothing, and is privation, or deficiency of a prerequisite quality in creation. Sin according to Saint Anselm prescribed a rejection of divine grace. Saint Thomas Aquinas decisively theorized that evil is subjective and the deficiency of Will in failing to attain actuality, or identity, then salvation. As with fellow scholastics, the thesis of Saint Aquinas on evil is privation. Nicholas of Cusa ([A.D] 1401-1464) echoed the nominalist rejection of realist belief in universal evil, under the influence of Neo-platonic idealism. Nicholas' chief work, "On Informed Ignorance" ([A.D.] 1440) imputes the independent principle of evil to god. All conceptions of god, evil, and the Devil are anthropomorphic, transcending imagination of being. God permits evil as privation in order for divine glory to manifest in transcendence of It.

The emergence of Zoroastrianism estimated around 1400 B.C., ascribes evil not as deity, but as a co-dependent power, dualistic in an exalted context of monotheism. Surviving sacred scriptures of adherents to the prophet Zarathustra (b. 630 [B.C.]) are entitled the Avestas. A surviving Avesta, actually a fragment of the compendium, is categorized into the Gathas, or odes to Zarathustra, Yasnas, or sacrificial liturgy pertinent to various demi-gods, and finally the Vendidad, dealing with ethics and ritual impurities. The Gathas are the first and foremost revelatory texts containing a responsive discourse between Zarathustra and his god, Ahura Mazdā. Zarathustra was a Persian zaofar (Avestan, "one who invokes," "one who pours") influenced by a profound sense of ritual activity and religiosity.

Later texts suggest, albeit of a legendary flavor, Zarathustra receiving divine revelation of Ahura Mazdā's division into six personified attributes called Amesha Spentas; "bountiful immortals." Ahura Mazdā existed as the head of a pantheon in the Indo-Persian divine triad known to theologians as ahuras. The other two divine entities of the ahuric triad were Mithrah and Varuna. The Vedic concept of ṛta (r.o.t.a.) ascribes law regulating an ordered multiverse, similar to the ahuras of asha, or 'righteousness,' emanating directly from Ahura Mazdā.

Fundamental to the problem and origin of evil in the Avesta is the allusion to the religion of the Avesta as dualistic, monotheistic, or a dynamic combination of both. Evil was a subject that profoundly exercised Zarathustra.

The starting point for the dichotomy of good and evil in Zoroastrianism proposes a radical ethical dichotomy personified in two opposing entities. The cause of choice again contributes to a proto-cosmic dualism transfiguring into eschatological monotheism. The ambivalent context of the Gathas alludes to the immaterial (menog) and material (getig) existences, pointing to an intentiality of creation. A developed Zoroastrian position on theodicy becomes clear in later Pahlavi writings.

Angra Mainyu (Pahlavi, Ahriman) is the Ahuric embodiment of the principle of evil in the Yasnas, accompanied by subsidiary antagonistic spirits. Angra Mainyu is an independent substance existing co-eternally with Ahura Mazdā in the Ninth Century Pahlavi text, Budahishn. The dialectic between good and evil is at once an exterior and interior struggle. In contrast to adherents of the Ahuric path, possessors of asha, are those stained with druj (lie), assisting Angra Mainyu, and are called drugvant.

Devotional theology in the Avesta augmented belief that Ahura Mazda initiated an ethereal line of continuity by creating such praiseworthy aspects of Itself. Such personifications of righteousness Zarathustra used proper names thusly; Vohu Manah ("good though"), Asha Vahiṣta ("best righteousness"), Spenta Armaiti ("good disposition"), and Haurvatat ("integrity"). In contrast, the holistic spirit Angra Mainyu manifested a subsidiary hierarchy consisting of: Aka Mainyu ("evil spirit"), Aka Manah ("evil thought"), Azi Dahaka ("avarice and avidity"), and Az, or Azi ("lust"). The maleficient acts of Angra Mainyu were constrained to the getig plane, thus is the material always in greater jeopardy than the merog.

Evil is conceptually existent in the menog yet only approachable in the getig. It is permissible from a contextual guise to see evil as parasitic, suffocating, and infectious as evil of Itself lacks corporeality. We are told in the Bundahishn that Angra Mainyu shaped his diabolical hierarchies from the substance of dark unmitigated æthyr. The Druj is the ideal embodiment of ultimate evil according to the Yasnas and Videvdad.

Personified by Angra Mainyu, Druj in canonical Zoroastrianism is the locus of malignancy and all contention. Angra

Mainyu in the Bundahishn is often depicted analogous to Druj, allegedly committed to obstruct the righteous material firmament, extolled as the world of *asha* (righteousness). To the Mesopotamian Pazuzu is attributed a chthonic corruption of theodicy. Pazuzu is imputed as a pale of evil in Sumerian and Akkadian mythology as patriarch of the spirits of the words. The son of the Sumerian devil *Hanbi*, 'lord of devils,' was postulated to antagonize the entity Lamaştu in ancient Akkadian vignettes, Pazuzu commanded the southwestern winds, depicted often with the body of a man, two pairs of wings, having the head of a lion or dog, a tail of a scorpion, and serpentine-like penis.

A further distinct novelty in diabolatry is the insidious corruption of Ba'al as maleficient. Etymology of the Semitic primitive stock stems from the root, *bá'āl*, "to possess." Therefore, the term implies ownership of real estate, possessor of a household and is so used in diverse applications of Semitic dialect. When the noun is applied as a prefix to deity, a sense of ownership or dominion is implicit in divinity. Thus did a variety of *Bá'àls* elicit special attributions. *Bá'àl Berîth* was the 'possessor of the Covenant,' Bá'àl Márqŏd was the 'possessor of ritualistic dance,' *Bá'àl Zebub* the owner and lord of the Philistine city of Ekron in connection to the ill health of King Ahaziah.

The corruption of Bá'àl Zebub became a novelty associated with disease-infested flies unto Philistine and Israel. The Septuagint corruption later vulgarized as Beelzebub is a phonetic dissimilation of Bá'àl Zebul ('zebel,' dung) in order to vulgarize the Canaanite deity as 'God of dung." Saint Jerome mistranslated the text as "dominvs muscarvm" (lord of flies).

The term *B'El* is the earliest form given as a national deity amongst Babylonian culture. In the Babylonian pantheon, B'El is distinguished as 'god of the earth' apart from Ea, 'god of the underworld,' and Anu 'father of the heavens.' In the Minoan, Phoenician, or Palmyrene urban centers, the sun was distinctive of the Bá'àl worshipped. *Bá'àl Hadad* appears the chief incarnation among the Assyrians. In ancient Canaan, methodology of Bá'àl worship is not obscure. Bá'àl was the chief proprietor of agrarian fertility, thus the lawful owner of agriculture. Worship of the Bá'àl diversifies according to place and circumstance. Noxious methodology of Bá'àl worship were seen by Hebrews as a degradation of Yahweh and elevation of Bá'àl in place of Yahweh.

Hebrews scorned the worship as lecherous religious fantasy. Subsequent to the division of Solomon's Kingdom into Judah and Israel, Hebrews led by the Temple Priesthood to distorted petitionary worship of Yahweh, sank further into Canaanite and pagan superstitions. It is feasible that such degeneration by the Hebrews consigned Yahweh to be addressed as Bá'àl, with the existence of such terms as Baalia in I Paralipomenon (Chronicles) 12; v.5-6.

The proper noun Asmodeus is evident in the Book of Tobit as a contentious spirit whom lusted after the human women Sarai, daughter of Raguel. According to Tobit III; 8 v.14, seven husbands of Sarai were slain by Asmodeus upon the night of wedlock. Later Hebrew and Chaldean expansions have Asmodeus rendered as docile after the marriage of Sarai to Tobias in addition to intervention from the angel Raphael on behalf of the two Lovers. King Solomon employed the innocuous demon with the assistance of Raphael in erecting the Jerusalem Temple. Haggadic legend connected the Asmodeus of Tobit with the unbearable bile of Ashmedai, a demon native to Rabbinic literature.

Hebrew Law forbade the use of ironclad tools (Exodus XX; v.26) in constructing the sacred Temple of the Israelites. The Masons, according to lore, could not fathom how to shape blocks of marble properly as the magi advised Hiram and his Masons to obtain the shamir, a worm capable of cleaving rocks with its touch. Solomon dispatched his chief, Benaiah ben Jehodah, to ensnare Ashmedai and elicit his knowledge of where to locate the shamir worms. Ashmedai succumbed to mortal trickery and remained to service the Temple until its completion.

The Testament of Solomon reveals that the *Ashmedai* mythos corresponds to representation of demons by their characteristics. Passages in the Talmud shed less light on the characteristics of *Ashmedai-Asmodeus*. Rationalist Theologians equivocate Ashmedai-Asmodeus with the Persian arch-demon Aeshma frequently mentioned in the Pahlavi text *Bundahishn* and the Zend'Avesta. Asmodeus-

Ashmedai of the Testament of Solomon seduces mortals to debauchery, enmity, and addiction, a striking resemblance to the unchaste deeds of Aeshma in the Bundahishn.

Azazel is the name of a being associated with the ritual of the Day of Atonement in Rabbinic literature. The High Priests, according to Leviticus XVI, presented to Yahweh sacrificial offerings of a burnt ram and two young goats. One goat and ram was slain before the Tabernacle as atonement unto Yahweh for the sins of Hebrews. The last goat was sacrificed in a glamorous and elaborate ritual offered to Azazel. The Priest laid his hands upon the goat and confessed upon it the sins of the Hebrew nations.

The petitionary goat, now laden with impurities was led astray and set loose into the isolate wilderness. As the epitome of impurities, Rabbinic literature interprets the etymology of Azazel as Azaz (rugged) and el (strong) in allusion to the rugged terrain where the sacrificial goat was cast forth. Modern scholasticism concludes, though retaining the orthodox lore of Azazel that Azaz'el belonged to hairy goat-like demons called the Se'irim. We have allusions to hairy goat-like demons in Leviticus XVI; v.8, II Chronicles Xi; v. 15, and Isaiah XXXIV; v.14, reaffirming the goat as a sacrificial sin offering carrying the impurities off Israelites into inaccessible terrain inhabited by hairy goat-like demons.

The cultural figure of *Azaz'el* is an object of fetish ascribed to penitent prayer in Rabbinic sacrificial ritual. *Azaz-el* is not a foreign cultural assimilation or the invention of a canonical Prophet. The Book of Enoch confirms Azaz'el as an antagonist in the classical Fall of the Angelic Hosts. According to Enoch's recounting and witness, Azaz'el brought iniquity to Mankind, teaching carnal Man the arts of combat, of constructing swords, spears, poisons, and shields, and the use of coasts of mail.

Azaz'el taught women to impart deceit, ornament the body, cosmetics, and eroticism. Azaz'el is possibly a degradation of Babylonian deities Mot, 'Uzza, or 'Azzael. In the Mandaean and Phoenician Pantheon, we have the promontory *rŏṣ'aziz* ("head of the strong") and the conjecture that the merging of āzāz, and él only would lead Us to far in archaic literature cited for this context. To fallow

Christian diabolatry, 'Ăzāz'él is no more than a demonic motif of the desert.

The tasks of the Klippotic powers are to cause entropy, to reverse the life process; as the Zohar says, "the end of all flesh has come before Me (Sammael);" for he, as the Evil Serpent, "takes away the souls of all flesh," that is he liberates them from matter. He is called the Angel of Venom, of Poison, of Death; for Sam means "poison" and El means 'angel.' His number is 131 that is trinity set between two unities, the whole adding up to 5 - the Microcosm. His world is now the Yetziratic World reversed; that is to say Assiah is the simulacrum, shadow, or image, of Yetzirah. Its three supernal Sefiroth are Tohu, the Formless, Bohu, the Void, and ChShK - Darkness. Its seven lower Sefiroth are seven hells.

Each of these ten Infernal Sefirot is inhabited by a host of demons, of which the first two orders are without form, the third is of darkness, and the remaining seven represent all human vices. The Klippoth of Malchut and Yesod are containers, cosmic filters from the world of natural elements. They are the more natural elements of human existence, emotions, unnatural desires, earthly principles; corresponding to the four tens and the pages/princesses.

Lilith is attributed to the demonic forces of Malchut and Yesod, ruling the "polluted of God," misshapen obsessions and demons who "flee from God." Nahema or Na'amah rules the Nahemoth, demonic agents responsible for exciting the human mind, causing unnatural desires and strange obsessions in exotic places. Nahema, Na'amah, is referred to mythically as the sister of Tubal Cain.

Yantra is a metaphysic device that brings the self to breach the restraints of the subconscious and dreaming world, to subdue elements of the phenomenal world. American scholar David Gordon White writes Yantras "...were at once divine and human genealogies, ritual and meditational supports, and models of and for microcosmic, mesocosmic, and macrocosmic reality, in which color, number, direction, divine name, vital breath, activity of consciousness, sensory organ, etc., were so many simultaneous proofs for the coherence of the world system they charted..." Yantra derives from the Sanskrit root, yam, geometric schema used as a mesocosmic medium to penetrate human consciousness and conceptual reality.

These geometric schemas are often sexual formulas, sometimes symbolizing Tantric sexual positions, more often symbolic of the Sun, Moon, and Lotus petals, representing the wisdom of kama, desire, or erotic interplay between Man and the divine. Klippotic Yantras, or talismans, are interplay between idea and image, thought and archetype, thus being an atavistic trigger for the Sorcerer to awaken extrasensory abilities.

Using talismans assists one to enflesh the divine with the bestial self – the subconscious merging with the waking mind, developing heightened levels of instinct, psychic ability, and eros. Through the psychic triggers of a Yantra, the magician reshapes himself/herself as an avatar of the Old Serpent, a manifestation of Chaotic Will.

The Lilith Grottos that are an exact vibration of the Kali Vidyas {esoteric spells, occult knowledge}, embodies the idea of time withdrawn into NOT, the shells of the dead worlds {Klippot} divided by time and chaos. As the dæmon of Malchut, LYLYT represents the mirror, the inverse chaos of the Cabalistic material realms, She, as Kali is the first to be divided into the Dyad, by both the noumenal sense and disruptive phenomena of time. She is Chaos in a single image, divided eleven-fold by the emanations of the ten Klippot, including Daath.

Kali, like Her Sumero- Babylonian & Hebraic counterpart, LYLYT, is the primal image of blackness, the echoing Void of Chaos, typifying death and negation in a meta-physic sense. The mystic breach that broke the manifested Sefirot, and created the husks of Klippot, is the primordial symbol of the Draconian undercurrent, represented by circle, and inverted triangle.

The Door of Daath, Veil of the Abyss, and the symbolism of the Abyss and Klippot pervades all esoteric traditions and mythologies. The place of the beginning of time and chaos, the origins of kala, typified by Kali and LYLYT, is the abyssal waters of the Deep. This chaotic metaphysical image is transferred to atavistic sigils which activate the sleeping psyche and subconscious, for Man to use in exploring the chaos of the blackness and the unspeakable terrors therein.

The ritual use of Vidyas to isolate and activate the psyche, and incur sensory-somatic-emotive deprivation brings the Adept to a state of carnal catharsis that is organic embedded in the human brain and genotype. Esoteric knowledge is latent within the human genome. These mystograms and the secret use of mantras, mudras, and Vidyas activate the unused portions of the brain, overtaking any psychic blockages with this catharsis, bringing the daring soul to the Mouth of the Abyss {Daath}.

Each of the eleven talismans represent Qlippotic hieroglyphs & eleven vibrations of Lilith in Malchut. Use the talismanic Grottos in conjunction with secret signs, mudras, and mantras typified by LYLYT and the Qlippotic orders. These Grottos are sexual in nature, symbolizing degrees of sexual gnosis and conjugation. They are mirrored by the most secret formula of sex magic, used in the fifteen Nityas of Kali and Lalita {another Tantric vibration of Lilith} described in the *Shaktisamgana Tantra*.

"He, O MahaKali, who in the cremation-ground, naked, and with disheveled hair, intently meditates upon Thee and recites Thy mantra, and with each recitation makes offering to Thee of a thousand Akarda flowers with seed, becomes without any effort a Lord of the earth."
- Karpuradi Stotra v.15 by Sir Arthur Avalon

Like Lalita, Kali has fifteen Nityas {Sanskrit 'eternities'}, but these correspond to the waning rather than the waxing Moon of the Lalita. The yantra mystograms supplied here above are based on descriptions from the *Shaktisamgana Tantra*. Some of the descriptions of the Nitya yantras in this work are missing, explaining their absence from the original Tantric text. The cryptic images and mantras should be contrasted with the Lalita Nityas and Yantras. While the Kali Nityas are inverted and forbidding, representing the Draconian undercurrents {the dead worlds, or Kabbalistic Qlippot} and the mantras have inimical natures, the Lalita Nityas are luminous, sexually playful and the mantras celebratory and devotional not wrathful.

The Talismanic Vortices of Lilith, eleven in number

associating the Klippotic Grottos of Lilith with the ten Sefirot including Daath. Each Lilith mystogram is derived from the Tantra Nityas of Kali, accompanied by a selected verse from the 22 verses of Sir Arthur Avalon's Karpuradi Stotra, adding to the sexually charged symbolism of Lilith's Qlippotic Grottos.

The ensuing lists of correspondences, orders, and cross-references of Qlippotic principles is based on the research of the old Hermetic Order of the Golden Dawn for magical use:

Klippoth Orders:

- **Thaumiel** - demonic powers seeking to destroy the unity of God.

- **Augiel** - spreading Confusion of the Power of God.

- **Sathariel** - work to conceal the perfection of God.

- **Ga'ashekelah** - seek to destroy or devour the substance and thought of creation.

- **Golohab** - attempt to destroy, or burn, these powers as well as what is ruled.

- **Tagirion** - demonic powers causing ugliness and groaning. A'arab

- **Tzereq** - the raw, emotional energy with which to overcome obstacles.

- **Samael** - represents the complete desolation of a fallen or failed creation.

- **Gamaliel** - the realm of polluted images that produce vile results.

- **Lilith** - representing all of the worldly pleasures.

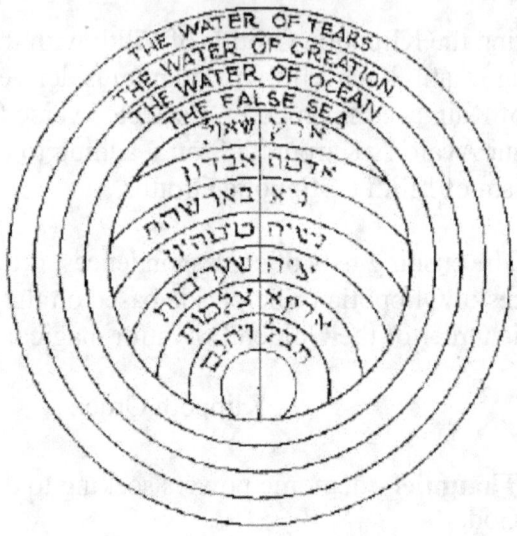

- *7 Shells of the Kingdoms of Edom ~ the 7 earths:*

- **Aretz** — Dry crumbling Earth

- **Adamah** — Reddish mould

- **Gia** — undulating ground, like the side of a valley

- **Neschiah** — Pasture or meadow land

- **Tziah** — Sandy or desert land

- **Areqa** — Earth

- **Thebel** or **Chaled** — earth and water

Adverse Powers beneath the Cherubim:

- **She'ol** — Depths of the earth

- **Abaddon** — Perdition

- **Titahion** — Clay of Death

- **Bar'Shasketh** — Pit of Destruction

- **Tzelmoth** — Shadow of Death

- **Shaari'moth** — Gates of death

- **Ge'hinnom** — Hell

22 Infernal Sentinels of the Sephirot and their dimensions:

- *Kether* **Thaumiel** The Fool; The Black Sun, Lord of the Klippoth World: Spirits of: Lufugiel, Mahaziel, Abraxsiel, Azazael, Thadekiel.

- *Chockma*-**Ogiel**-Magician, the Averse Planets; Spirits of: Dubriel, Lufexiel, Alhaziel, Chedeziel, Itqueziel, Golebriel.

- *Daath*-**Typhon**-Gateway to Qlippoth.

- *Binah* **Sateriel** Universe, Lucifer; Hidden Knowledge, Concealment, hides in shadows, invisibility, darkness, Guards the Qlippoth realm from the profane. Spirits of: Saturniel, Asteriel, Reqraziel, Tagariel, Abholziel, Lareziel, Abnexiel.

- *Chesed* **Gasheklah** Wheel of Fortune-Brings wisdom to the path unseen, brings change and continual motion, beginning of initiation, Illumination of the black flame towards path of becoming gods. Spirit of: Malexiel, Gabedriel, Chedebriel, Amdebriel, A'othiel, Theriel.

- *Geburah*-**Golachab** Tower-Destruction, war, confrontations, powers and strength, abilities gain, maker of the tools of magic and the power behind it. Spirits of: Gameliel, Barashiel, Ebaikiel, Lebrexiel.

- *Tiphereth*-**Tageriron** Sun; hidden powers of the klippoth, seeking darkness and power, Dragons of Tagarironare shades of energies of darkness, creation and power, creating servitors, bring things to form Spirits of: Mephisophiel, Gobraziel, Rebrequel, Taumeshriel, Raqueziel.

- *Netzach*-**Oreb Zaraq** Time; Control and command astral forms and shadows, night or ravens to a specific goal, includes dreams, projection and the astral, masters magick powers, dragon powers. Spirits of: Helebriel, Satoriel, Baruchiel, Reteriel, Refreziel, Labreziel, Astoriel, Reptoriel.

- *Hod* **Samael**; Hanged Man-The will of Lucifer embodied within, to become a god, to know darkness and light, a dimension that protects dragons from the light of earth, absorb knowledge and wisdom, the truths of Klippot, to sacrifice what's not needed, the pathway of the Black Sun, initiation of dragon kind. Spirits of: Sheoliel, Molebriel, Libridiel, Afluxriel.

- *Yesode* **Gamaliel**; High Priestess-Shadows and dark beings live here, where magic is being formed, sex and lust, the moon of Lilith, the place where there are tests, place to draw power and energy, night magic, dreams and seduction. Spirits: Idexriel, Materiel, Lapreziel, Gedebriel, Alephriel, Labraeziel

- *Malchut* **Lilith** Empress-Five accursed Nations-Earth, humans, animals and fairies, the physical world of chaos, where Algol does his will, magick manifests here:

Five accursed Nations:

1- **Amalekites**-Aggressors

2- **Geburim**-Violent ones

3- **Raphaim**-Cowards

4- **Nephilim**-Sons of the Fallen Angels

5- **Anakim**-Children of chaos, Anarchists

Spirits: **A'ainiel, Thauhedriel, Molidiel, Heteriel, Nobrexiel.**

Dagdagiron Capricorn Devil; Manifestations, influencing someone, gain power over someone, gaining authority, success in something, overcome obstacles, creating façades, the past, restricting someone confusion spells. Sexual fetishes and death, night, manifestation, creative power, initiator, power to create or destroy.

Behemiron Aquarius, Star; The Bestial Ones)-Banish gossip, wishes come true, to bring confidence, getting what you desire, know others plans, desires of someone, brings chaos, changes, the unexpected, revealing something unknown, destructive, breaks barriers and blocks, strange energies, occult knowledge, awakening energies. Forms of force and harsh manifestations, change, essence of the black flame, and the eye of set of awareness manifestation of the Luciferian current.

Neshimiron Pisces, Moon - Malignant Women)-Revealing secrets, revealing the hidden, to undo someone, psychic powers, finding spies, undermine some-ones spell, to capture someone, to hide something, bindings, escape from an issue, confine evil, free an issue, karmic release, invisibility, finding someone, revealing deception, finding the truth. Manifestation of the female current, breeds other dragons, bestowing power of female dragons that seek their power, sex magick, awakens the Luciferian essence.

Bairiron Aries, Emperor; Sending things, sparking anything, glamour magic, perception and reality, shape-shifting, alterations, beginnings, initializing, war, attacking, conflict, aggressive magic.
,power and authority with balance, communication and wisdom, the antichrists will made manifest on the earth, mastery of earth and Qlippoth realms, helps write spells and gain spell ideas, empowers with energy, to make manifest.

Adimiron Taurus; Hierophant, Storage of energy, multiplying anything, find lost things, to bring damage to something, new abilities, to gain anything you desire, make things disappear or reappear, to acquire something, returning anything. ,wisdom and information and secrets of the Qlippoth realm, finding hidden knowledge, astral travel, dream work, brings magic storms, using dragon powers to create and destroy.

Tzelladimion Gemini; Lovers Telepathy, mind control, influence thoughts, travel, communication, sending messages, immediate environment, find information, getting magic books, spell crafting, gossip finder, learning magic, change something, alter thoughts, , curses, bind someone, banishing, protection
alteration magic, quicken something, make things move, awakening the spirit of Luciferian magic to become gods, to be initiated, sacrifice the old for the new, Hidden knowledge of the gate to the Qlippoth, to direct ones magic, awaken magic, learns the art of Qlippoth magic, bringing its knowledge within, this path is opened by the words: Zazas Zazas Nasatanada.

Schechiriron - Cancer; Chariot - Protection, hidden issues, bring an end to something, graves and the undead, ancient magic, finding what was lost, servitor creations, spirits and shadows, demons, weather magic, storm raising, altering the past, the past and history, to preserve something, emotional issues, nature magic, human being fully awakened, to acquire and attain the art of Qlippoth magic, sending out magic forces and will, guidance on the path of the Qlippoth, journey to attainment, guide the magick, expand visualization, manipulating energies.

Shelhabiron Leo/Strength/Lust and sex, creating anything, messengers, ego magic, law of chance, illuminates issues, awakens energies, stimulation of something, gaining power, wish magic, primal energies, revealing anything, burns problems away, union of forces or powers, lust and desires, the essence of Luciferian magic, to bring completion to something, to induce and sustain realization, instinct and strength, the will of the magician, to bind energies to a goal, motivating the self, the process of a goal, to attain what one desires.

Tzephariron Virgo; Hermit; Healing, to purify, cause sickness and ill energy, make others do what you want, repair energy, animal magic, to alter something, chakra magic, to contain something evil for protection, to bring change to something, to hide something, summon energies, unnatural pathway to the Qlippoth realm, to achieve a goal, to seek illumination, the connections between things in magic, finding associations to things, to awaken inner power, awakening to the Qlippoth realm, finding knowledge within that realm, find others strengths and weaknesses, to seek dark powers and consume the light.

Obiriron Libra; Justice, Destructive energy, to form new beginnings, create links, to combine a force, to create strife, make arguments, attack something, catch a thief, attract something, domino effect, sending forces elsewhere, creating the opposite of something, balancing anything, makes spells end, to draw in energies to form and send, refine and manipulate powers, to prevent things from moving too quickly, destroy energies that try to harm.

Necheshethiron Scorpio; Transformation, the dead, creating fear, recreate something, banishing, reflect something, bring to an end, make someone obsessed, occult powers, invisibility, hiding anything, altering something, research, secrets and hidden information, destructive, shadow magic, wraiths, shades of the dead, necromancy, raising the dead, darkness, night magic, death magic, astral magic. Death, Shedding the unwanted, gain powers, become more powerful, getting rid of issues and the past, restoration magic, overcome something, inciting chaos, bring things to an end or its death, to find important information, gaining draconic knowledge, guides you on the path of power, guidance of the Qlippoth realm.

Nachashiron Sagittarius; Make something grow, expansion of an issue, astral travel, dream magic, prophetic, to learn new magic, energy manipulation help, movement of something, freedom, connecting with aliens, learning tarot and astrology, manipulating something, cosmic magic, gaining knowledge, remote viewing, revealing the truth of an issue. Temperance, Transmutation and shape-shifting, transformation from one thing to another, development, to make things manifest, counterattacking, bring the best or worst out of something, incite passion, gain strength, to aid in focusing, to bring balance, lord of war and storms, understanding the Qlippoth, and working with dragons, rules over the dead, magic to become godlike.

12 Zodiacal Princes of the Qlippoth:

- BAIRIRON; so called because they are derived from the Fourth Evil Force; viz, Samael the Black. Their colors are dull and black; and their form is that of a Dragon-Lion.
-

- ADIMIRON; whose colors are like dam1 blood, mixed with water and dull yellow and gray. Their form is that of lion lizards.

- TzELLADIMIRON; whose colours are like limped blood, tzelil,2 bronze and crimson. They are like savage triangular-headed dogs.

- SCHECHIRIRON; whose colors are black, and their form blended of reptile, insect and shell-fish, such as the crab and the lobster, yet Demon-faced withal.

- SHELHABIRON; whose colors are fiery and yellow and their form like merciless wolves and jackals.

- TZEPHARIRON; whose colors are like those of earth, and their form is partially living yet decaying corpses.

- OBIRIRON; whose colors are like clouds and their form like gray bloated Goblins.

- NECHESHETHIRON; whose color is like copper, and their forms like that of a most devilish and human headed insects.

- NACHASHIRON; whose colors are like serpents, and their form like dog-headed serpents.

- DAGDAGIRON; whose colors are reddish and gleaming, and their form like vast and devouring flat-shaped fishes.

- BEHEMIRON; whose arms are derived from Behemoth, and their colors are black and brown, and their forms like those of awful beasts, like hippopotamus and an elephant, but crushed flat, or as if their skin was spread out flat over the body of a gigantic beetle or cockroach.

- NESHIMIRON; whose colors are of a stagnant gleaming

watery blue, and their forms like hideous women, almost skeletons, united to the bodies of Serpents and Fishes.

Chthonic Guardians of Zodiacal paths in Qlippoth:

- Aleph **Amprodias**; Vampiric Slyphs

- Beth **Baratchial**; Poison of God

- Gimel **Gargophias**; Lemurs

- Daleth **Dagdagiel**; Babalon

- Heh **Hemethterith**; The Herd

- Vau **Uriens**; The Bloody Ones

- Zayn **Zamradiel**; The Clangers

- Cheth **Characith**; The Black Ones

- Teth **Temphioth**; The Flaming Ones

- Yod **Yamatu**; The Scratchers

- Kaph **Kurgasiax**; The Smiters

- Lamed **Lafcursiax**; The Clayish Ones

- Mem **Malkunofat**; The Deep Ones

- Nun **Niantiel**; The Brazen Ones

- Samekh **Saksaksalim**; The Creeping Ones

- A'ayn **A'ano'nin**; The Lying Ones

- Pe **Parfaxitas**; The Arsonists
- Tzaddi **Tzuflifu**; The Bestial Ones
- Qoph **Qulielfi**; Malignant Women
- Resh **Raflifu**; The Hagglers
- Shin **Shalicu**; Tannim
- Tau **Thantifaxath**; Ghouls

Of the Infernal Trinity before Samael:

Qematiel, whose form is that of a vast black-headed Dragon-serpent and he uniteth under him the force of Kether of the Internal and Averse Sefiroth.

Belial, a black, bloated Man-dragon. He who denied God; and he that uniteth the force of the averse Chokmah.

Othiel or **Gothiel**, a black bloated man-insect horrible of aspect; his breadth greater than his length; and he uniteth the force of the averse Binah.

Samael the Black. All of these are of gigantic stature and terrible aspect.

4 Qlippotic Rivers:

North- Earth; **Acheron**

East- Air; **Cocytus**

South- Fire; **Phlegethon**

West- Water; **Styx**

32 Tunnels of Set:

11. Fool: **Amprodias**; To make things unaware, astral travel, Qlippoth guides, a gift of dark power, dangerous issues, to see mistakes, to know ahead of time, guidance, freedom.

12. Magician: **Baratchial**; energy work, elementals, gaining powers, directing forces, magick of all kinds.

13. High Priestess: **Gargophias**; inner alchemy, hidden knowledge, dark energies, opening the unseen, awakening, initiation, psychic powers, portals and gateways.

14. Empress: **Dagdagdiel**; the darker aspects of nature, dark Fay magic, creation of servitors, manifesting into existence, ancient power.

15. Emperor: **Tzuflifu**; controlling others through magic, powerful energies, to influence someone, make things go your way.

16. Hierophant: **Uriens**; reveals things, connector of other forces, helps with magic ritual, guide to the underworld.

17. Lovers: **Zamradiel**; to illuminate what direction to go, the truth of something, division of anything, weapon to protect.

18. Chariot: **Characith**; astral travel, protection and defense, to make invisible, spoken spell craft, memory manipulation, altering the past, great powers.

19. Strength: **Temphioth**; Telepathy, helps to control powers, power to destroy, protection, to gain more power, to gain awareness, to see past a façade, see others' motives.

20. Hermit: **Yamatu**; dark powers gain, wisdom of the black flame, to gain knowledge, learn from, secret workings, shadow magick, time magick, illumination, revealing anything.

21. Wheel of Fortune: **Kurgasiax**; the fate of an issue, its destiny, to bring change to something, to evolve, spiraling downward, bad luck, synchronicity.

22. Justice: **Lafcurisax**; justice and defense, to bring judgment, curses, teaches dark magick karma of something, repelling magick, deflection, to unbalance something.

23. Hanged Man: **Malkunofat**; Inner alchemy, astral magick, chakra work, getting psychic powers, reveal deception, hide things, sacrifices, brings death.

24. Death: **Niantiel**; Necromancy, learning the art of evocation, death magick, shadow powers, guide in the underworld, bringing changes into something, sex magic.

25. Temperance: **Saksaksalim**; Reality morphing, altering anything, keeping magic working, switching energies, switching souls, drawing and swapping powers.

26. Devil: **A'ano'nin**; Binding spells, banishing energies, sex magic, restricting others, bondage, glamour magick, dark energies and magick, blocks, releasing them.

27. Tower: **Parfaxitas**; To destroy something, bring an end to, brings chaos, secrets revealed, to know the truth, to bring surprise, weirdness, the odd, revenge.

28. Star **Hermetherith**; access to the universal mind, other dimensions, occult knowledge, the black flame awakened, illumination, darker Fay magick.

29. Moon: **Qulielfi**; Dream walking, astral magick, dark workings, to discover the hidden, psychic abilities, expose deception, awaken third eye.

30. The Sun: **Raflifu**; can make things dry up, or make things grow, to radiate a certain energy, glamour magick, to unfold new powers.

31. Judgment: **Shalicu**; Breaks barriers, and limitations, to expand something, awakening into dark power, to bring termination, to stop a spell from working, to resurrect something.

32. World: **Thantifaxath**; To consume someone's magick, to annihilate something, to create a servitor, or to destroy one, ending something, or beginning something.

POPULAR MEDIEVAL AMULET TO PROTECT THE MOTHER AND CHILD AGAINST ATTACK BY LILIT DURING CHILDBIRTH.—FROM *Sefer Raziel*, AMSTERDAM, 1701.

VIII

Origins of Lilith

In the philosophy of the Hebrew Kabbalah, Lilith corresponds to the daemon of Malchut in the Klipphot. Lilith annihilates litanies of inhibitions in the human psyche. Etymological origins of Lilith independent of Jehovian-Semitic templates point to the Sumero-Babylonian Lilû, which translates to 'a demon equivalent to a male vampire.' Derived from Sumerian, Lila refers to 'wind,' or 'storm.' Opting for Akkadian translations, scholars suggest Lalu, also Lûlu as 'lecherous,' and 'wandering.' Few people know that Lilith's prehistory predates Jewish iconology. The Creature has been much maligned not only in Jewish and Christian scripture, but also in the esoteric ideologies that permeate "sexually free" modern "magical organizations."

From the Akkadian Lilitû and her Sumero-Babylonian compliments, Ardat-Lili, Idlu-Lili, and Lamaştû, derives the Semitic LYLYT {Lilith}. The Lilitû primarily feasted upon women and children, referred to by the terrified inhabitants of Ur and Babylon as night-ghosts that roamed the deserts away from populace. Pictographs from 800B.C. to 500B.C. Babylonia depict "Lilith" in the company of snakes and other abominable animals, keeping with themes of her malevolence in Babylonian pottery, Persian and Jewish amulets and in the Qumran scrolls.

The night-ghosts here evolved into the Jehovian mythopoeia seeping into the Christian paradigms of diabolatry. Isaiah 34:14 in the Vulgate refers to "he-goats," "hairy beasts," again carried over from Judaic paradigm. The Vulgate thusly reads; "Et occurrent daemonia onocentauris, et pilosus clamabit alter ad alterum; ibi cubauit lamia, et inuenit sibi requiem." Isaiah 34; xiv-xv refers to Lilith as the 'Screech Owl.'

Classic Rabbinic commentaries favored a demonic being that frequented ruins, in the form of screaming ghosts or monstrous birds – "screech owls." The two linguistic roots; Leila {Arabic for 'night'}, and y'lala, "to howl." Contemporary Rabbis believe Isaiah is talking about devils, entities themselves based on entropic phenomena; thus their howling or 'screaming' presences are the true Spirits of the Ruins. Yehezkal Kaufmann believes that *lilit*, or LYL, linguistically is associated with the Semitic word for night; layil. (Y. Kaufmann, The History of the Faith of Israel, Tel Aviv: Bialik, Jerusalem, and Dvir, 5736, vol. 1, p. 428.) S.R. Driver suggests that the lilit is a type of bird on this link between the word *lilit* and the Sumerian storm spirit. (G.R. Driver. 1959 "Lilith: Isaiah XXXIV: 14," Palestine Exploration Quarterly, 91:56-57) He argues that the *lilit* is a bird of the night which moves in a circular fashion, in both the Bible and ancient Sumerian, it was called a *lilit* from the root *lili* or *luli* indicating a spiral motion of a storm.

Another linguistic root of Semitic-Akkadian origin and source for Lilith is the root *lalu* or *Lûlu*. King Assurbanipal's extensive library retained thousands of tablets, many of which are full of conjurations whose purpose is the exorcism of various demons. Lilith the Babylonian demon often appears as a member of an infernal triad including "*Lilu, Lilitu,* and *Ardath-Lili.*" In Sumerian, these names derive from the word "lil," meaning spirit. In Akkadian, they perhaps derive from "*Lalu*" (plenty, or excess) or *Lûlu* (lust, promiscuity). Here we have the following traits of Lilith in a much more finalized linguistic puzzle;

- night; leila
- howling; y'lala
- demonic spirit; lil
- storm; lil
- circular movement; lil, lul
- spiral movement; luli
- opulence and excess; lalu
- lust, promiscuity, and debauchery; lulu

Lilith in the Talmud is a roaming wild demon of the Qlippoth; her features are linked to rabbinic concerns about modesty. Women's hair as a symbol of their sexuality was deeply problematic for Talmudic rabbis. To them it represented promiscuity in the face of Ecclesiastic purity and patriarchal dominance. According to the Talmud, revealing "the hair of a woman is immodest." In the opinion of the Rabbis, long hair recalls the hair of the demon Lilith, she grows long hair like Talmudic depictions of Lilith, and she crouches when urinating like a hairy beast, and becomes a cushion for her husband for she is astride him during sex. Long flowing and loose hair on a woman was associated with malevolence and promiscuity, as women were embarrassed to go out with their long hair flowing in front of the men. The Babylonian Lilitu was ready at hand as a cultural iconoclast who concretized and gave shape to deep rabbinic fears and Jewish superstitions.

In the Alphabet of Ben-Sira, Lilith aspects of a myth are forged together to tell the primordial tale of Jehovah's two attempts to find a suitable "help-mate" for Adam {Ish}. In this mystical text, Lilith is assigned demonic status; "sleeping with the Great Demon." Lilith's Qlippotic origins are subsumed from earlier sources into a dominant Jewish patriarchal narrative.

Now in this olde Jewish tome, the 'independent' Lilith the Great Demon, presumably asserting her religious independence from Yahweh. It is to no avail; the tome redomesticates Lilith because she still joins herself with Adam and to other men while they are asleep. Consider the origins of succubi and of "fallen angels" – these mishappen creatures imply error in divine creation. Is "God" at fault?

Remaining in the realm of Jewish {and later Medieval Christian} myth, Lilith arouses sleeping men with erotic dreams, copulates with them and steals their semen in order to impregnate herself. From this human seed, she begets demons, succubi, and other malignant beings; all these races of mishappen creatures take great indulgence in causing sexual obsessions and mental diseases to man. Lilith with the "chaos demon" replaces the chthonic, Qlippotic she-demon whose source is connected to procreation and patriarchy.

The Ben-Sira text constructs a misogynistic origination myth for feminine evil, an absorption of diabolatry and demonism into Lilith and all women themselves, in earlier Zoharic and Talmudic sources, Lilith was the swirling, demoness of entropy an alternative power to the Godhead. Consequently, by the time the root LYLYT in Hebrew derives from Lilith myth is deconstructed in classical form, she is reduced to a promiscuous woman gone wild, the archetype of a divorced woman; a person created by Yahweh who voluntarily "disobeys." We can go looking no further than to the Torah, the Christian "Olde Testament," and Pauline Letters to the Church at Corinth to witness the malediction against women; past, present, and future originating in the texts we have briefly discussed before exploring the darkest tunnels of your own psychic scars and erotic nightmares:

"A woman who becomes pregnant and gives birth to a son will be ceremonially unclean for seven days, just as she is unclean during her monthly period. On the eighth day the boy is to be circumcised. Then the woman must wait thirty-three days to be purified from her bleeding. She must not touch anything sacred or go to the sanctuary until the days of her purification are over. If she gives birth to a daughter, for two weeks the woman will be unclean, as during her period. The she must wait sixty-six days to be purified from her bleeding."
 - Leviticus 12:2-5

"Do not approach a woman to have sexual relations during the uncleanness of her monthly period."
 - Leviticus 18:19

"Let your women keep silence in the churches: for it is not permitted unto them to speak; but they are commanded to be under obedience, as also saith the law, and if they will learn anything, let them ask their husbands at home: for it is a shame for woman to speak in the church."
 - Corinthians 14:34-35

"And I find no more bitter than death the woman who is a snare, whose heart is a trap and whose hands are chains. The man who pleases God will escape her, but the sinner she will ensnare....while I was still searching but not finding, I found one upright man among a thousand but not one upright woman among them all."
 - Ecclesiastics 7:26-28

"Of the woman came the beginning of sin, and through her we all die."
- Ecclesiastes 25:22

"The birth of a daughter is a loss." - Ecclesiastes 22:3

"You shall not covet your neighbor's house. You shall not covet your neighbor's wife, or his manservant or maidservant, his ox or donkey, or anything that belongs to your neighbor."
- Exodus 20:17

"If a man sells his daughter as a servant..." - Exodus 21:7

"As in all Churches of the saints, the woman should be subordinate as even the law says...for it is shameful for a woman to speak in church."
- 1 Corinthians 14:34-35

"Let a woman learn in silence with all submissiveness. I permit no woman to teach or have authority over men. She is to keep silent, for Adam was formed first then Eve, and Adam was not deceived but the woman was deceived and became a transgressor."
- 1 Timothy 2:11

"For if a woman will not veil herself then she should cut off her hair, but if it is disgraceful for a woman to be shorn or shaven, let her wear a veil...for man was not created from woman but woman from man. Neither was man created for woman but woman for man."
- 1 Corinthians 11:6

IX

Grottos of Lilith

The Yantras are derived from descriptions based on the Shaktisamgana Tantra. These Grottos are used in conjunction with the **Rite of Lilith**. Sexual force is the polarity that functions as continuity between the Sefirot and Qlifot, symbolized dualistically by a lightening flash and coiling serpent upon the Tree and its Nightside. Concerning the dark absences, the negative way, behind the Sefirot, Adepts who issued the Cabala mistakenly branded the Klipphot as "evil" and averse to the Tree of Life, when in reality the Klipphot is the shadow of existence, what Buddhist Adepts call sunyata, the dark absence of intrinsic objectivity. This noumenal Reality shadows the Cabalistic phenomena of existence.

The retention of sexual fluid strengthens etheric fluid, called *prna*, which is a reservoir where the existence of the self is annihilated. These tentacles of bio-energy, immaterial fluid, can be opened through various practices of "sex magic," and ritual use of the Qlifot, the dead shells of creation. One of the most closely guarded secrets of retention of the sex fluids and etheric fluid is symbolized by the open and closed Draconian Eye {*Ayin*}.

Klippoth, according to the Adepts whom issued the Kabbalah, were to anti-powers that shadowed concealed in these grottos, or chambers that reflected the Sefirot, hence the "demonic" attributions to the unfathomable depths and their denizens. The grottos, tunnels, and chambers discovered by Adepts navigating the Klippoth saw as I do, that the ancient sagas of evil, and its paraphernalia of tomes, devils, hells, death, and *apocalypse* are disfigured shadows of the Abyss. The primordial denizens of NOT hold unfathomable secrets of the Klippoth tunnels, tomes, and grottos that are grasped by the racialist cursed occultists that can breach the disfigured shadows of the Void.

The Grottos of Lilith number 11, adumbrating the 10 Sefirot as shells, husks of divine vibrations that merged time and space, the archetypal & material worlds, the noumenal planes with phenomenal existence. The 10 Orders of the which is ascribed a "false Sefira," as the illusion of all knowledge, the Door to Death and the cessation of physical incarnation in order to breach the bounds of the Abyss. All ancient mystery traditions and their paraphernalia of evil are dominated by primordial symbols of a Tree, Serpent, Sun/Star, and Water. The deities and sometimes zootypical beast-human hybrids that peopled the primordial races believed that the creative Serpent initiated Mankind with its wisdom, after rising from the Depths {the Waters of the Deep, or deluge, from which Tiamat and Apep issued forth}.

The Klipphot that are the 11 Grottos are the gateways to the Abyss, they are the adumbrations of the Sefirot with Daath, acting as webs of Ophidian gnosis that interconnect the 22 Tunnels of Set. The Grottos, or Orders of Klipphot acting as chthonic vortices, contain their own classifications of imagery and thaumaturgy. The 11 Klipphotic grottos are the shadows of non-being obscuring the divine and material emanations of being proper to the Tree of Life.

It is this closely guarded inner secret of the Typhonian undercurrent that represents the orgasm, {A = Typhon} which is an allegorical 'death' of the Self. This orgasmic "Crossing" is an allegory of non-being, what Buddhist Adepts refer to as sunyata, formlessness that transcends perception, existence, and non- existence. I encourage you to study the *Prajnaparamita Hrdaya* {Heart of Perfect Wisdom} Sutra of the Mahayana Buddhist Adepts. This tract and its esoteric mantra, used in many Tibetan Tantric sects, contains a fascinating discourse of the nature of "crossing the Abyss" and realities associated with the metaphysical event.

The new Life in this equation, the meta-physic I, is fertility in its most exalted sense, a glyph of the fulfillment of the Great Work, symbolized by a Serpent {Yod} issuing forth from the Abyss, developing the poisonous {Klipphot} sexual spermatozoon, resulting in incarnation – a rebirth {O = Osiris risen} thus capitulating the endless cycle. The 11 Grottos of Lilith intrinsically also functions are Klipphotic extensions of Malchut, 11 are the symbolic Dukes of Edom, for eleven is One Beyond the Ten Qlifot, include Daath emanations, One Beyond the Sefirot, thus giving way to the Infernal and Averse Grottos.

The Queen of Malchut, LYLYT, divides Herself into 11 'curses,' 11 Grottos of chthonic gnosis. Sex is the natural elixir and modifier through which one tunnels through the Grottos, for they adumbrate the unbroken Creations. The Grottos are the shells, worlds of pure chthonic vortices, touched by Artisans like H.R. Giger, Soror Laailah, Andrew Chumbley, H.P. Lovecraft, Kenneth Grant, & Austin Osman Spare, and countless others of the Black Lodge.

The vivifying of these 11 vortices is the sole aim of all esoteric systems of sex magic. The immaterial fluid aroused in the depths of our being, called tsing in Taoist ritual sex, can be activated in every aspect of life, not solely through sexual activity. The grottos of Lilith, as extensions of Klipphotic Malchut, serve as reservoirs of subtle bio-energy, when misappropriated becomes manic, a common result in Klipphotic workings.

One finds it possible to "leap," or "vault" into different grottos, and advanced undertakings of sex magic by traversing the 22 Tunnels of Set, the negative lights of OB and OD. In Rabbinic lore, LYLYT {Lilith}, the insane night-ghost, or Mad Hag, become demonized as an eclipse of Light, wrought with menstrual impurities {menstruation was viewed by Orthodox Rabbis as horridly impure}, a distorter who opened the Tree of Life to the chaotic depths.

LYLYT opened the Tree of Life to the Breech, the Klipphot typified by Daath the "eleventh Sefira." Thus, the 11 Grottos of LYLYT are the breaks, the adumbrations in the Cosmos that opens vortices where the denizens of the Klipphot may interact with the human species & vice versa. Lovecraft correctly wrote of extra-dimensional breaches in space and time, similar to the grottos and tunnels of the Klipphot. Many of his tales represented monstrous hordes of the Chaos, and windows through which phenomenal existence was destroyed, similar to the apertures of the Klipphot. Many religions and Mystery Traditions alike forbid contact with the Grottos, in fear that one's consciousness would be swallowed in the swamp of NOT.

Lost souls through Arte, drugs, sex magic, and sensory deprivation have gazed into the unfathomable Deep, into the black swirling Mouth of the Abyss, and saw the shades massing for dark influx into Malchut, into our unbroken world. Sensitive souls have scryed, painted, and recoiled in utter horror at the sight of the swirling hordes massing behind the Veil of NOT.

The eleven *Grottos of Lilith*, and the twenty-two Tunnels of Set can appropriate these vortices, making it possible for one to "leap" to different planes of monstrous forms and the gaping Void of dreams and subconscious landscapes. Sex, and sexual imagery alone is the entry point to each of the eleven Grottos. Mythic and zoomorphic imagery dealing with sexual prototypes, {Lilith, Succubi, Spermatozoon, Phallic Godforms, etc} swarm in human tales as haunters of the Deep, and other primeval mutations.

The Grottos then acting as primeval reservoirs retain this atavistic imagery in the hells of human subconscious. Such are the darker pathways of Red Magic. Eleven signifies then the One beyond the 10 Sefirot, the infernal Yoni at the Breech of the Tree, the Evil Woman allegorically 'behind the Tree who tempts Mankind.'

The sexual devices and iconography of the Grottos are concealed due to the primeval, "unnatural" sexual prototypes {such as Succubi, Incubi, Lycanthropes, and other monstrous hybrids of subconscious and flesh} lurking in the Grottos. Sex represents a Draconian, primeval eclipse of the soul where the self is isolated and the subconscious activated. Thus, through sex and the lower machinations of the subconscious, the Klipphot, all its grottos & tunnels becomes activated in human consciousness.

The eleven grottos of the Klipphot that function as emanations of Lilith and her demonic race are represented by the eleven scales of the Old Serpent who opened the Breech of the Tree of Life. This Breech of the Tree of Life, its grottos, tunnels, webs, and tomes, have been explored by such Adepts as H.R. Giger, H.P. Lovecraft, Abraham Stoker, Kenneth Grant, Sir John Woodroffe {Arthur Avalon}, Arthur Machen, Charles Stansfield Jones {Frater Achad}, Aleister Crowley, Austin Osman Spare, Andrew Chumbley, Soror Nema, Soror Laailah and few others who have dared.

Malchut begins the process of vibrations that adumbrate the

Sefirot, transmitting the Draconian undercurrent through each of the eleven Grottos. Each of the Grottos are cosmic & special vortices, where noumena and phenomena negate the other. It may be useful to consider the Grottos and their interconnecting tunnels as dream cells for the subconscious, embedded in the human genotype as primeval codes that isolate the instinct & dreaming mind. Each Grotto is named after an Order of Klipphot for which it adumbrates, and reverses the affect.

Each of the twenty-two tunnels, which are archetypal transit pathways, interlock with the eleven Grottos, their powers and iconography originating at the Mouth of Daath. Daath is the event-horizon that binds the entire schema of the Klipphot to the Draconian undercurrent, enfleshed in the subconscious of Mankind thousands of years ago only to be reawakened in dreams, dimensional travel, sex, and chaotic necromancy.

The name and sources used for the Grottos, Tunnels, and Orders of Klipphot I gathered from Kabbalah Denudata by S.L. MacGregor Mathers {trans.}, On the Kabbalah and its Symbolism by Rabbi Gershom Scholem {1965}, Karpuradi-Stotra by Sir John Woodroffe {London, 1929}, Complete Golden Dawn System of Magic by Israel Regardie {Falcon Press, 1995}, & Nightside of Eden by Kenneth Grant {Skoob, 1977}.

The templates for the Yantras derive from descriptions in the *Shaktisamgana Tantra*. The Grottos effectively are designed as Yantras of Lilith, eleven vibrations of Malchut that mirror the fifteen Nityas of Kali. Each Lilith Yantra is derived from the Tantra Nityas of Kali, accompanied by a selected verse from the twenty-two verses of Sir Arthur Avalon's Karpuradi-Stotra, adding to the sexually charged symbolism of the twenty-two Typhonian tunnels, and Lilith's Klipphot Grottos. Listed with each of the eleven Lilith Grottos, are the infernal names of each order of the eleven Klipphot, Daath included. Magical evocation and psychosomatic use of each Grotto is available to the most daring, due to the primeval nature of the Klipphot and its blackest magic.

The grottos, tunnels, and vortices of the Klipphot contain the most primeval and chaotic forces, while it is possible to transit and vault to different Grottos and Tunnels of Lilith in the space-time continuum, it is wise not to imagine the Breech of the Tree completely mirroring the Sefirot. As a human physiology has various arteries, capillaries, veins, and nerves, the Klipphot contains a similar decentralized network of Grottos, tubes, tunnels, vortices, and dream dimensions. Once opened through the Mouth of Daath, each Grotto contains its own vortex that swallows ones soul in NOT if one fails utterly in casting the infernal alignments. Use these rituals and meditations as a catalyst to open the Klipphot and the Breech of the Tree of Life. Engage in sexual intercourse with partner or begin acts of autoerotic masturbation.

Grottos of Lilith

"Hitherto shalt thou come, but no further: and here shall thy proud waves be stayed."
- Job 38:11

Below each of the eleven Lilith Grottos are listed the infernal names of each order of the eleven Klippoth, Daath included.

Genuflect to the East, South, West, North, and then west again always going counter to the direction of Kronos {counterclockwise}.

<u>Face direction of Luna</u> {Moon}. Give Sign of Lilith and Sign of Laylah. Or substitute with Signs of personal choice. Touch genitals.

Gaze skyward toward the Firmament: Formulate the Cross:

- Touch the brow and vibrate: NA'AMAH
- Touch the breast and vibrate: LILITU
- Touch the left shoulder and vibrate: AYSHETH ZENUNIM
- Touch the right shoulder and vibrate: AGRAT BAT'MAHLAT
- Touch the genitals and vibrate: LYLYT
- Place the palms of the hands together upon the chest, in benediction vibrate: LILIT MALKAH HA' SHADIM

Formulate Triangle.
Give Sign of *Isis Ascendant*.

Recite:
> *veharetz hayta tohu vavohu vekhoshekh al-pnei tehom veruach elohim merakhefet al-pnei hamayyim*
> **And the earth was without form, and void; and darkness was upon the face of the deep. And the Spirit of the Hosts moved upon the face of the waters. Malchut Her False Sea the husks of Light reflecting the Four Great Rivers of Nod, the seven Infernal Habitations, the seven fallen earths.**

First Grotto Lilith: LYLYT
Meditation:
A horrible grinding sound, maddening...in which the Firmament, which is æther, grinds down into matter. Your body afire with a crimson shadow; hurled into wondrous torment and blackness...the stench of human flesh comes. The bowels of little children are torn out and thrust into the gaping mouth of a Serpent...poison is dropped into your eyes. Lilith, a black coiling Serpent, crawling with filth, running with open sores, eyes white as the moon, scales on Her serpentine skin, fangs, her nose eaten
away, her mouth a gaping maw, coils about your shadow- body. You are consumed by the Serpent.

First Grotto Lilith: LYLYT

Second Grotto Gamaliel: GMLYAL
Meditation: An endless sea of ebon and ruddy depths...the waters of Daath. The All-Seeing Eye of Set behind you in the Void of NOT. Your shadow is cast into the Deep, suffocating...losing all sense of subjective identity until you suddenly hear the baying of a monstrous Beast penetrate the Abyss. Your shadow finds it-self sitting in a vast barren wasteland...the desert of Daath...the shadows of the ripples of the sand torment you with whispers of unspeakable fetishes and fantasies. You behold the beauty of the earth in its biological death, the beauty of your Soul in its desolation. You will break...you continue to hear the millions of mad voices in your animalistic brain coalesce into one Obscene Bestial Voice. A naked Obscene Woman with the legs of a hairy beast riding upon an Ass moves toward you. Around the Woman Riding upon the Ass you see races of Bull-men...your mind and consciousness transfers to the Ass as it stares into your shaded eyes. You become the Obscene, succumbing to bestial instinct.

Second Grotto Gamaliel: GMLYAL

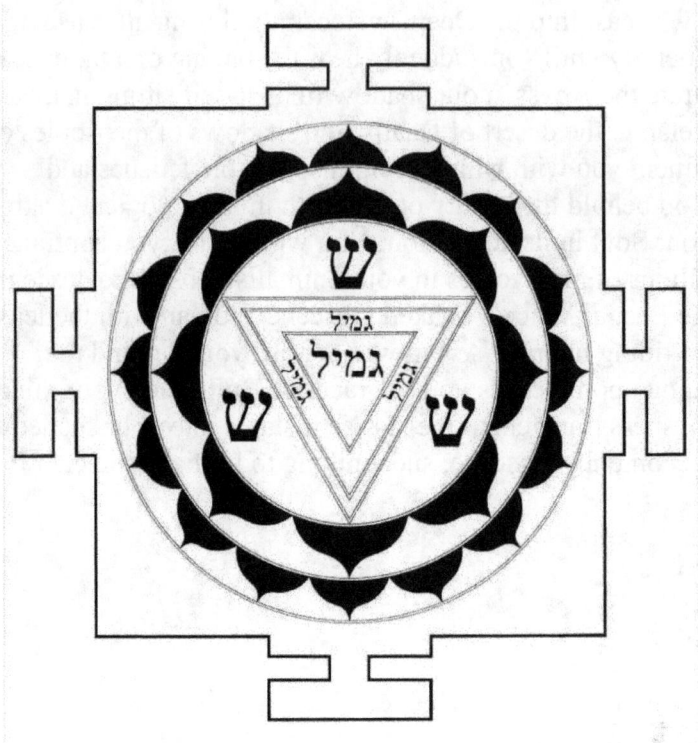

Third Grotto Samael: SMAL

Meditation: Succumbing to bestial instinct you mount the Obscene Woman...realizing in unnatural rapture that all of creation is a lie, and a failure. Your new Bestial eyes behold a black Sun set in the ruddy skies...this is the Desert of S--t {Set} where Time is NOT save a shadow of consciousness, a pale reflection of eons. A vast expanse of Shadow covers all existence...you find yourself again transforming as the shades of the desert of NOT..the abominable races...your bestial awareness is overwhelmed by a great crimson light the color of blood. All the ethers, all you perceive around is consumed by a great crimson Light...your shadow self turns and behind you is a vast network of caverns, grottos, tunnels, caves of ruddy dull material, stretching as far as you can behold. You see a vein in this giant labyrinth...realizing it is a vast river of blood...with fumes, smoke, and ash rising into nothingness...four angels with burning scales ride upon four horses at the bank of this river, their bodies burning each riding upon a white, red, black, and dark olive horse respectively. You come to smell the burning scent of the ethers...the Four Horse Riders burn into smoke...all around you burns in a great Black Flame .... your shadow body is now a burning crimson shadow...you realize all the failures of creation reach NOT. There is nothing..but the Black Flame of gnosis.

Third Grotto Samael: SMAL

Fourth Grotto

A'arab Tzereq:**AARB TzRQ**

Meditation: The Great Black Flame subsides in the crimson smoke of the Klippoth of Hokmah...all is ash. The crimson smoke parts you behold with your shaded eyes the swirling destruction of souls and angels dissipating in the fumes & smoke of the Great Black Flame. Again the Veil of the Klipha parts...once again you behold vast labyrinth of caverns, grottos, tunnels, caves of ruddy dull material, stretching as far as you can behold...before you this time lays a monstrous volcano penetrating into the ashen heights...swarms of millions and millions of demon-headed ravens surround this volcano in the form of a giant swastika. Streams of fire emit, brilliant black and ruddy plumes of grey and red...one of the demon-headed ravens flies into your body...you feel yourself lifted...flying into the swarms of demon-ravens circling the abyssal volcano..over the endless labyrinth...your breath is the fire of madness...the millions and millions of demon-ravens abandon you ... you see with your demonic- avian eyes a peculiar light in the maw of the volcano...into the maw you fly...behold the myriad deaths of the 32 ethers...behold the ruins of Eden and Binah.

Fourth Grotto
A'arab Tzereq:AARB TzRQ

Fifth Grotto
Togaririm: ThGRYRVM
Meditation:
In the chthonic depths are you renewed in Abaddon Perdition and destruction of Binah Out of a great sea of burning coal and ember you see Leviathan, who is numberless Dragon forms united together so that each of his scales is like a separate Serpent arise surrounded by titanic black amphibious beasts unbearable to look at...the beasts emit strange croaking and bellowing utterances that crack the firmament beneath your shadow body...a giant groan envelopes the dimension around you, the revolting amphibious beasts flopping and crawling about you speak in utterances you begin to comprehend...the continuous Groan is the bellowing of Leviathan, you heard the word **Chozzar** as one endless intonation...the infernal name dies out as the Groan divides into millions and millions of voices speaking as NOT: once, the Ancient of Days was NOT and silence. the Time of Nothing is a closed Eye. Behold the Chaos of the Sefirot...the husks their Alignment." You withdraw into your shadow body... experience the intolerable ache of the Soul's separation from Itself. You voice replies to the echoing dimension that is being swallowed up by a Great Dragon Leviathan "I am the snake that devours the spirit of Man with the Lust of NOT. I am the sightless storm in the night that wraps the world about with desolation. Chaos is my name, and thick darkness. Know thou that the darkness of the earth is ruddy, and the darkness of the air is grey, but the darkness of the soul is utter blackness." Peer into the Eye of Leviathan...behold the ashen pylons of Geburah and its thunderous Titans.

Fifth Grotto
Togaririm: ThGRYRVM

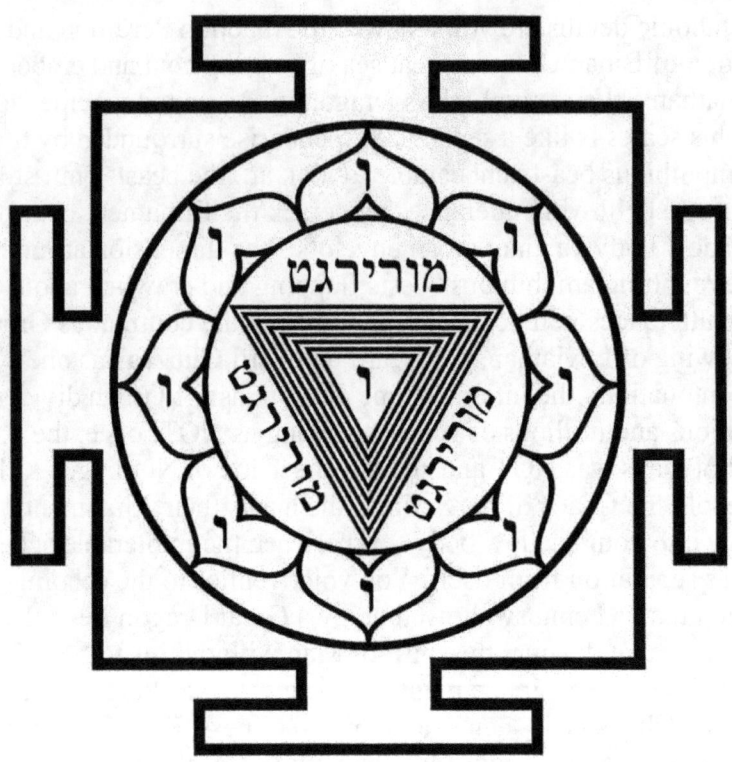

Sixth Grotto Golachab: GVLAHB
Meditation:
Transiting through a Tunnel of thick burning scarlet scales, your shadow body enters the husk of Geburah...you see the Four Beasts of the Apocalypse kneeling before an enormous throne...which is empty. Your shadow body rushes into the shell like a great plume in the burning winds that surround you...that which you see is the alignment of Severity and its Chthonic pylons...an empty throne heralded by the Four Great Beats of the Apocalypse symbolizes the mysteries of the unfinished Klipphot...Tetragrammaton is no more, consciousness in Man overthrown by the Burning Serpents who enflesh desire and knowledge inside dreams & nightmares...There is no God but Man...all around your body is burning scarlet scales, shed by Flying Serpents ... eons appear before you in reverse succession all judged before the Empty Throne to be dispersed in the Fires of Severity...the decapitated Head of a Serpent is placed upon the Empty Throne...the Headless Serpent coils around your body of shadow...the ethers are bound up in the Klipphot, also the tunnels for the Order of the Sefirot is a corruption of the Tree of Life, the workings of the Klipphot align the eons for they alone retain the knowledge of the nexus between space and stars, the spaces between the spaces...behold the Headless Serpent leading you through the tunnels to the husk of Chesed.

Sixth Grotto
Golachab: GVLAHB

Seventh Grotto
Ga'ashekelah: GAaShKLH
Meditation: Transiting through the tunnels of the Klipphot, you are lead in your body of living shadow by black giant beast-cats & three titanic monsters of impossible shapes with the heads of cats kneeling before a great black Sun in the middle of a triadic formation of three azure moons...a terrible hissing thunderous with anger & severity spews emanates from this great black Sun: "the light of Mercy is gone asunder in Man...Man feeds upon the names of the Most Infernal Serpent he fears the powers of the Pentagram and Triangle, he knows Not the name 393...its formula aligns the Twin Star." You are the Disturber...all thought and creation is a waste issued forth from the dead shell of Has--d...Matter and Form have no dispersion...the Firmament is the failure of the Blind One...all is dispersion these are the qualities of FORM...NOT disperses all thus are these Grottos the true emanations....for when the Eye closes – what exists but the Nexus between time and space... ....**Ga'ashekelah** curses the eons with Shapeless horrors that pulse in your blood & the dimension around you...your shadow Form is hurled into transits through tunnels that bear unspeakable shapeless abominations leading to the chthonic alignment of Hod...

Seventh Grotto
Ga'ashekelah: GAaShKLH

Eighth Grotto Sathariel: SATARYAL

Meditation: Transiting out from the pylon of Daath, your living shadow coils about the tunnels of Klifot into the non-alignment of Hod...the Chaotic Universe of Hod fragments with the rushing of Air twisting the stars and constellations into shapeless horrors of NOT...your living shadow is dispersed into Concealers and Destroyers whose forms and appearances are as gigantic black veiled Heads with Horns, and hideous eyes seen through the veil, surrounded by blackened centaurs...through the cyclopean Eye of one of your fragmented Beast-Shapes you behold Noxious blind **Azathoth** ... surrounded by dancing mindless and amorphous creatures. **Azathoth** divides the Firmament into spiral black vortices gnawing at the failed Sefirot between time and space...space itself becomes an illusion you realize you are **Azathoth** and that all the Klipphot is a reflection of IT....sucked into one of **Azathtoth's** black spiral vortices you behold the Klipha, Netzah...

Eighth Grotto
Sathariel: SATARYAL

Ninth Grotto Oghiel: AaVGYAL
Meditation: Transiting through the black spiral vortices of the Qlippotic Tunnels your living shadow-Form is hurled into the Klipha, Netzah...about your living shadow-Form are all manners of fantasy of flesh and sexual obsession...wild terrestrial landscapes abound before you consisting of vast geometric cavernous dwellings, and mountainous structures of burning earth...a nameless stench rises forth....about you crawling mists arise and reveal **Oghiel**...the crawling mists hiss into your mind unspeakable fetishes & fantasies, attaching themselves unto lying and material appearances...the crawling mists slowly morph into Black Vaporous Giants with shrieking serpents twined round them...the mystery of this Grotto is the truth of the Qlifot: there are no tunnels, the Coiling Serpent raises Her head out of Daath, all the Sefirot are ill-alignments of Qlifot and their calamities ...He who makes the Sefirot is the Great Deceiver...your shadow-Form morphs into the non-being of Oghiel...following the crawling mists you transit through the Chthonic Tunnels to the Klipha, Yesod the Tenth Grotto of LYLYT...

Ninth Grotto Oghiel: AaVGYAL

Tenth Grotto Thaumiel: ThAVMYAL
Meditation:
Transiting through the amorphous tunnels, your shadow-Form is hurled into the Grotto of Lilith that adumbrates Yesod...you find your shadow-Form isolated and utterly alone...there is NOT but you and YOU ALONE....this is the Lie and the horror of the Grand Architect of the Universe, the Maker of Illusions to disperse the loneliness of NOT...before you appears a nameless shadow morphing into various prophets, Magi, Magister Templi, and Avatars...morphing endlessly next into the Bicephalous Ones; and their shapes are those of Dual Giant Heads with bat like wings..they have not bodies for they are mindless shapes that seek continually to unite themselves unto the bodies of other beings and forces....you behold the Bicephalous Ones morph from the nameless shadow continuously until you behold the LIE that is **Thaumiel**...who whispers with millions and millions of shrieking Voices that the Shaper of the Sefirot has created Falsehood ..."the Supernal Triad is but a reflection of the Qlifot in its entirety" spoke **Thaumiel**...the Arcanum of the Qlifot is thus revealed...divinity in its isolation, enfleshed in FORM in MAN to know Itself...."that which is below is not like that which is above, that which is above is not like that below..." spoke **Thaumiel**...you realize that before you is not **Thaumiel** but your own shadow-Form divided .... blackness ...blackness intolerable before the breaking of the shells, Chaos ... Chaos is the reflection of the Abyss...all is NOT...you are utterly alone & isolated...

Tenth Grotto Thaumiel: ThAVMYAL

Eleventh Grotto Naamah: NAAMH
Meditation:
A living shadow coils about you...morphing into the shape of a voluptuous maiden with crimson tinged skin...covered with rotted lilies and roses...supported by countless myriads of scaled demons swarming about Her...upon her vagina, breast, and brow is the secret Mark of the Old Serpent...She wears a crown of the stars of Orion, the Pleiades, Leo, the Pole Star, the stars of Scorpio, Virgo, and Draconis ... hissing, She gently whispers in a sibilant voice: "*I, Naamah, guide thee through the husks of failed Creation, I renew through death that is NOT...unless one is in the shadow of the earth, he cannot see the stars. So, also, unless he be hidden from the light of the Supernal, he cannot behold Lilith.*" Here, do you abide in unalterable blackness and deformities of the Klippotic Grottos and their denizens, utterly at peace...an intolerable ache fills you beyond ecstasy, beyond thought, beyond being itself to unite with **Naamah** in Her Grotto...for every sexual act produces a mirrored effect on every planes...all these visions are the Falsehood of Sefirot...every Sefira is a shell of a Klipha...this is your soul pure black...**Naamah** gives suck from her paps to sorcery, and theft, and rape, and gluttony, and murder, and tyranny, and to the nameless Horror which Judaic racialist black magicians wrongly attribute to the Qlippot...these things are the instinct of Man...vibrating into the Grottos throughout the maddening tunnels...

Eleventh Grotto Naamah: NAAMH

X

Lailah and Naamah

Among a congregation of angels, one serves as the midwife of souls. Lailah is the Angel of Conception. When a man and his wife conceive a child, God directs Lailah to seek out a certain soul hidden in the Garden of Eden, and command it to enter a drop of semen. At first, the soul refuses, for it still remembers the pain of being born, and it prefers to remain pure untainted by physical existence in Malchut, the material realms of creation. Lailah compels the soul to obey, and that is when G.O.D. decrees what the fate of that sperm will be, whether male or female, what the soul's social position, physical conditions, mental constitution will be, and so on.

After the soul is bade to enter the sperm, Lailah turns around and places the soul in the womb of the mother. As the infant grows in the womb, Lailah places a lighted candle at the head of the unborn infant, so he can see from one end of the world to the other, as it is said, His lamp shone above my head, and by His light I walked through darkness {Job 29:3}. Lailah watches over the unborn infant for nine months, teaching the soul the secrets of angels and demons as well as the souls own history.

The Angel of Conception recounts the soul's history, the secrets of Qabalah, and forgotten languages and ciphers of angels and demons, as evil inclinations lose their power over the soul at this time. Before the soul incarnates into a body, he or she is given an oath to Lailah to keep the soul immaculate, lest the soul is taken back. Lailah leads the child into the Garden of Eden and shows him the sublime ones with crowns of stars on their heads. So too does Lailah lead the child to the netherworld and show him the castigations of Gehenna. And when the time has come to be born, the angel extinguishes the lamp of conception, and brings forth the child into the body.

The moment the child emerges from the host mother, Lailah strikes the newborn above the lip, causing it to cry out. And at that instant, the infant forgets all it has learned in previous incarnations and its time in the meta-physical or ethereal realm. This is the origin of the mark on the upper lip, which everyone bears. Lailah is a holy guardian angel, who watches over the child all of its days. And when the time has come to take leave of this world, it is Lailah who comes to the child saying, "Do you not recognize me? It is time now. I have come to take you from this world." Thereupon Lailah leads the departed soul to the ethereal abodes, where the soul renders an accounting before G.O.D., and is judged according to its merits during the incarnation.

The name Naamah or Na'amah (Hebrew, meaning pleasant) appears in the Torah as the daughter of Lamech, sister of Tubal-Cain and half-sister of Jubal. (Genesis 4:22) Naamah may or may not also be the wife of Noah or his son Ham. The meaning of her name is argued among Judaic scholars; it refers either to her virtuous nature, 'pleasing' to YHVH or to a proclivity for idolatry singing' pleasant' psalms to pagan idols.

Naamah is regarded as the inventor of divination and prostitution. Naamah is a figure in Jewish mysticism. She is often regarded a succubus and fallen angel and is generally regarded as an aspect or relation of Lilith. Naamah is said to have engaged, like Lilith, in intercourse with Adam.

Naamah appears in the Zohar (Zohar I 55a) as one of the four angels of prostitution, one of the mates of the demon Samael. Her other three associated succubi of prostitution are Lilith, Eisheth Zenunim, and Agrat Bat Mahlat. (Book of Jasher Chapter 5:15) In Zoharistic Kabbalah, Agrat Bat Mahlat also is one of the four succubi of prostitution, the mates of the demon Samael. If you consider Mahlat and Agrat as proper names and bat as "daughter of" (Hebrew), Agrat bat Mahlat translates 'Agrat daughter of Mahlat.' If Agrat is used alone, or with variations (Agrath, Igrat, Iggeret). Iggeret means in Hebrew, 'letter or missive' while 'agrah' means 'reward.'

Mahathallah, is likely the correct transliteration of *Mahlat* meaning in Hebrew 'deception' or 'illusion.' Agrat bat Mahlat could be translated as Agrat 'daughter of illusions, bringer of deception' or 'reward for deception Naamah is historically identified with the daughter of Lamech. According to scholar Robert Graves, this Naamah is a counterpart to the one who appears in Genesis 4:22 and she is regarded, like her mortal counterpart, as a patron of prostitution and music. Naamah is often named as the mother of the demon Asmodai, the consort of the Lesser Lilith; Lilith and Samael's brood. In Zoharistic Qabalah, Naamah's fellow succubus Eisheth Zenunim is also one of the four angels of prostitution, including Lilith, and Agrat Bat Mahlat.

These four succubi are also known as the Four Queens of Hell or the spouses of Satan. Author as Donald Tyson refer to them as manifestations of Lilith. Agrat Bat Mahlat rules Salamanca (western quarter), Naamah rules Damascus (eastern quarter), and Lilith rules Rome (northern quarter). The southern quarter is controversial, since it is assigned to Egypt instead of a Biblical city, and the name of the ruler is unclear, usually identified by Jewish Cabalists as Mahalat, mother of Agrat, or Rahab instead of Eisheth Zenunim.

Seventeenth century theologian John Gill identified Naamah instead with the name of the wife of Ham, son of Noah, whom he believed became confused in subsequent translations with Noah's wife. Naamah is also relevantly a city of Canaan, listed in Joshua 15:41, as having been conquered and settled by the Tribe of Judah. The city of Naamah a major tributary of the Canaanite royal city of Makkedah.

Even more significantly is Naamah, an Ammonite wife of King Solomon, and mother of his heir, Rehoboam, according to both 1 Kings 14:21-31, and 2 Chronicles 12:13. She is the only one of Solomon's wives to be mentioned, within the Tanakh, as having borne a child. In contemporary Gnostic Qabalah, Nahemah is the klippot corresponding to the sefirah Malchut.

The Rite of Naamah in its canon of ritual erotica, it is an operation of Qlippotic working, for the archetype of Naamah is sex and deception. Naamah as the lesser Lilith is embodied by metaphysical and ethnic origins of diverse ancient cultures. Adored and feared by mortals as the Sumerian Lilitu {also the Hand of Inanna}, Babylonian Lamashtû {Daughter of Anu}, Akkadian *Ardat lili*, the Hellenistic Hecate, or the Hindu Kali, it is She who enshrouds over our eyes the Veil of deception. Naamah is the mythic inventor of prostitution, the driving legend behind Mary the Magdalene, who was not a simple street prostitute. Those who transcend psychosexual

modes of deviance, and overcome religious memes will breed new genotypes to a social class better fitted to control their environments, a new psychology, and a new code of genetics completely unknown to contemporary Man.

Naamah's primordial whispers are worshipped in music across cultures in the works of the Medieval Maestros to the most depraved contemporary "rock" bands, frail beauty-Divas prostituting a latest cosmetic product to deceive the real waifs of beauty, in the scratch heroin needles of those whose nightmare reflects perfect Beauty, in the consensual rape of teenagers posing upon their digital and downloadable altars of self-adoration {think Myspace}, Naamah is the face in the bulimic puke of would-be- doll-girls in Hollywood behind a masochistic society. Her legends, as Lilith's, produce only those whose veins retain Her Imperial blood.

XI

Rite of Naamah

By the sign of the Le Dragon Rouge, by the word of l.a.y.l.a.h. and the Arcanum of the Sarcophagus...
being the Kabbalistic invocation of the Demon of Deception and Prostitution

c. 2003 Arizona desert.

Acquirements :
Red robe {Cloak or garments}
11 red candles: {symbolic of the 10 Sefirot, and the hidden Sefirah Daath, of the Kabbalistic Tree of Life}
Owl
feather
Chalice
Red wine
Athame or instrument to draw blood {women may use menses}
Myrrh, Sulphur, Storax & or Abramelin incense
Myrrh Oil
Bell

other devices to exalt the Spirit and stimulate the workings of the rite are left to the creative ecstasy and will of the individual

I Time :
Naamah's Rite must only be performed on the night of the New Moon, or on Samhain {Halloween} night. Never at any other time. The Rite lasts 24 hours, one full day and night.

II Preliminaries :

- Purification and consecration: Abstain from any and all sexual activity one full week; 3 days prior to the Rite, 3 days after the Rite, and day of.

- Fasting: Fast from sunrise to sunset completely from food one full day prior to the Rite and during the Rite.

- Day and Night of Rite: Do not speak at all. Keep silence from now until conclusion of Rite. Sunrise: Meditate in the sunlight according to personal custom and religious conviction for one full hour. If possible stay outside and secluded during the day until Sunset: bathe ritually in salt.

III Purification and Consecration :

Sunrise: keep silence, abstain from all sexual activity, and keep silence save for recitations during Rite, remain in seclusion until conclusion of Rite. Sunset: bathe ritually in salt water {again}.

- Enter ritual chamber robed/clothed in black. The Naamah Rite is done outside in natural setting, take caution to ensure seclusion and privacy.

- Genuflect and perform 9 full prostrations.

- Purify and consecrate the Sanctuary area or Chamber of the Rite, conduct the Greater Banishing Ritual of the Hexagram. Myrrh or Sulphur incense should permeate the entire sanctuary area or chamber. Light and arrange 11 red candles in a circle.

IV Sigil of Naamah :

The following ritual motions represent a withdrawal of prana, of intrinsic physiological energy, and rising of kundalini.

Stand erect in center of chamber/sanctuary. Take up Athame/bloodletting instrument and chalice while you are facing the West; introduce it above then so below, then to the IV corners, before you, behind you and at both sides. Genuflect to the East,

South, West, North, and then West again always going counter to the Direction of Kronos tracing the Ourobouris {counterclockwise}. Return instruments to altar.

Face direction of Luna {Moon}. Give Sign of Lilith and Sign of Naamah. Or substitute with Signs of personal choice.

Ring Bell 1 x 3 x 3 x 3 x 1 to ward to summon the spirits under authority of Naamah. Genuflect.

Face West. Touch in succession: Genitals, heart, left eye.

Gaze skyward toward the Firmament:

Formulate the inverted Triangle:

Touch the left shoulder and vibrate *Eisheth Zenunim*

Touch the right shoulder and vibrate *Agrat Bat*

Mahlat Touch the genital and vibrate *Na'amah*

i - describe a circle about the crown of the head (thumb between index & medius)
ii - thumb between index & medius (as before), describe cross in the form of an 'X' upon the brow
iii - as before, describe cross in the form of an 'X' upon the left temple

iv - as before, describe cross in the form of an 'X' upon the right temple
v - as before, describe cross in the form of an 'X' upon the left breast
vi - as before, describe cross in the form of an 'X' upon the right breast

vii - as before, describe cross in the form of an 'X' upon the genital

Rite of Lilith

Recite:
veharetz hayta tohu vavohu vekhoshekh al-pnei tehom veruach elohim merakhefet al-pnei hamayyim
And the earth was without form, and void; and darkness was upon the face of the deep. And the Spirit of the Hosts moved upon the face of the waters.

Malchut Her False Sea the husks of Light reflecting the Four Great Rivers of Nod, the seven Infernal Habitations, the seven fallen earths.

Draw near to me, come descend.. BAIRIRON Draw near to me, come descend.. ADIMIRON

Draw near to me, come descend.. TzELLADIMIRON

Draw near to me, come descend.. SCHECHIRIRON

Draw near to me, come descend.. SHELHABIRON

Draw near to me, come descend..TZEPHARIRON

Draw near to me, come descend.. OBIRIRON

Draw near to me, come descend.. NECHESHETHIRON

Draw near to me, come descend.. NACHASHIRON

Draw near to me, come descend.. DAGDAGIRON

Draw near to me, come descend.. BEHEMIRON

Draw near to me, come descend.. NESHIMIRON

The people walking in darkness have seen a great light; on those living in the land of the shadow of death a new Moon has dawned.

For She has rescued us with the dominion of darkness and brought us into the kingdom of the Serpent She loves.

This is the verdict: the Light of the Sun has been hidden, Her Kingdom has come into the world, and men love darkness instead of light.

Lilith Queen of Malchut said, "I am the Abyss. Whosoever follows me will fall forever into the false sea."

Face the location of the Moon and recite
before me Samæl behind me Thaumiel above me Oghiel below me Othiel
at my right hand Satoriel at my left hand Gamaliel Cover left eye with left hand and recite: at my death Qematiel

SHE, broken Light of God, shadow of Alpha and Omega, Lilith, Queen of the Concealers, Hinderers, Disputers, Burners, Breakers in Pieces, Disputers, Deceivers, Dispersing Ravens of the Burners, Nehemoth, and the Obscene.

Cover left eye with left hand and recite:
By the Seven Infernal Habitations of the dead worlds:
She'ol the Depths of the earth, Abaddon Perdition, Titahion the Clay of Death, Bar Shasketh the Pit of Destruction, Tzelmoth the Shadow of Death, Shaari'Moth the Gates of death, Gêhinnôm the Valley of Slaughter. Draw near to me..come descend, Lilith!

V Shir Ha'shirim :
Read aloud, Recite Jewish translation of Shir Ha'shirim, the biblical Song of Songs, Song of Solomon {Latin, Canticum Canticorum }.

VI Invocation of Naamah :

Come descend, thou dæmon-Queen of Malkuth Queen of Bar'Shasketh Mother of Harlots and Abominations of the earth Demon of Desolation! I call for Death I will for Death!

Come descend Bride of Samæl Demon of Tempest and Lust!

Come descend Screech Owl, Howling Cat, Tortuous Serpent! I call for Death I will for Death!

Come descend Mare of Night Owl of Darkness!

Come descend End of all Days End of all Flesh!
Come descend Queen of Gêhinnôm Queen of Zemargad! I call for Death I will for Death!

Come descend ABEKO I call for Death I will for Death!

Come descend AMIZU I call for Death I will for Death!

Come descend BATNA I call for Death I will for Death!

Come descend BATH ZUGE I call for Death I will for Death!

Come descend BABYLON I call for Death I will for Death!

Come descend GILU I call for Death I will for Death!

Come descend IZORPO I call for Death I will for Death!

Come descend KALI I call for Death I will for Death!

Come descend LAMIA I call for Death I will for Death!

Come descend PARTASAH I call for Death I will for Death!

Come descend SATRINAH I call for Death I will for Death!

Come descend LAMASHTU I call for Death I will for Death!

Come descend ARDAT- LILIT I call for Death I will for Death!

Come descend LA-KAL-IL-LI-KA I call for Death I will for Death!

Come descend KI-SIKIL-LIL-LA-KE I call for Death I will for Death!

Come descend KI-SIKIL-UD-DA-KAR-RA I call for Death I will for Death!

Come descend NAAMAH I call for Death I will for Death!
Come descend BITUAH I call for Death I will for Death

Touch in succession: Genitals, heart, left eye.

VII Conclusion:

Take up owl feather. Owl is the silence of the masques of madness, the hiding of the spirits. Face direction of Luna.

 Inscribe Hebrew name of NAMH נעמה with owl feather, completely fill chalice with red wine. Bleed the left hand, arm or region of the body, drip a drop of blood in wine-filled chalice. Engage in languid, undulating sexual activity building to orgasm and ejaculation of sexual fluids. Drip sperm, or ova, into wine-filled chalice then drink completely. Give Sign of Harpocrates {Sign of Silence}. Perceive the entry into the psyche burning spheres of deep crimson, bring thyself to a dark flash of ecstasy and gnosis of the Cross and Grail, of Christ and the Magdalene's suffering experiencing apotheosis. Behold with thine ethereal clairvoyance the deep crimson hue of ruddy Crosses about the chamber of the rite, or amidst thine bestial venue.

 Experience the arousing sensations of blood rushing throughout your body; hear its resounding echo course amidst the confines of the flesh. Envision a great crimson Shadow enflamed with carnal energy in front of you, engulf your entire perception of being into this shadow. It is hellish and haunting, seductive and erotic, thrilling every drop of your blood into ecstatic frenzy.

 Merge yourself and faculties with the Shadow you have evoked before you, engulf the essence of your blood into its black and haunting formlessness. Experience and smell the sensations of your blood uniting with the essence of yourself as a new entity. There is only this experience, you are of the nature of this

Shadow. Visualize your body a formless Shadow of great blackness, enflamed with the sounds of the rushing of the blood, seething between flesh and bone.

Circumambulate thrice counter-clockwise, tracing the Ourobouris around thee; Genuflect with each passing of the West. Return to center of the chamber. <u>Do not conduct banishing, purification rites</u>. Exit.

Bibliography

Adlington, William (Eng. trans.) The golden ass: being the Metamorphoses of Lucius Apuleius (1566) Macmillan New York, 1915.

Benko, Stephen Pagan Rome, and the Early Christians Indiana University Press, 1986

Birnbaum, Lucia Chiavola Black Madonnas: Feminism, Religion, and Politics in Italy ToExcel Publishing 2000

Carr. David M. The Erotic World: Sexuality, Spirituality, and the Bible Oxford University Press, New York, NY U.S.A. 2003

Crowley, Aleister. The Commentaries of AL, New York: Samuel Weiser, Inc., 1975

D'Este, Sorita Hekate: Keys to the Crossroads - A collection of personal essays, invocations, rituals, recipes and artwork from modern Witches, Priestesses and Priests ...Goddess of Witchcraft, Magick and Sorcery Avalonia London, U.K., 2006.

Dumars, Denise & Nyx, Lori The Dark Archetype New Page Books
Franklin Lakes, NJ, 2003.

Ehrman, Dr. Bart D. Lost Scriptures: Book That Did Not Make It into the New Testament Oxford University Press, New York, NY U.S.A. 2003

Galland, China. Longing for darkness : Tara and the Black Madonna
Viking New York., 1990.

Gimbutas, Marija The Language of the Goddess Thames & Hudson, London, U.K., 2001.

George, Demetra Mysteries of the Dark Moon: The Healing Power of the Dark Goddess HarperCollins San Francisco, CA 1992

Hurwitz, Siegmund Ph.D. *Lilith: the First Eve: Historical and Psychological Aspects of the Dark Feminine* Daimon Verlag Einsiedeln, Switzerland. 1992

Jameson, Anna *Legends of the Madonna* Houghton-Mifflin, New York, 1895.

King, Karen L. *Gospel of Mary: Jesus and the First Woman Apostle* Polebridge Press, CA U.S.A. 2003

Koltuv, Barbara Black Ph.D. *The Book of Lilith* Nicholas-Hays, Inc. York Beach, ME. 1986

Father Martin, Malachi. *Decline and Fall of the Roman Church* Secker & Warburg, London, U.K. 1982

McGinn, Bernard *The Flowering of Mysticism {Presence of God: a History of Western Christian Mysticism}* Herder & Herder Frieburg, Germany, 1998

Miravalle, Dr. Mark, STD (Editor) *Mary: Coredemptrix, Mediatrix, Advocate-Theological Foundations* Queenship Publishing Santa Barbara, CA 2005

Monte, Cedrus N. *"On the Black Madonna: An Interview with Andrew Harvey"* excerpt from Gustafson, Fred (Ed.) MoonlitPath: Reflections on the Dark Feminine Nicholas-Hays, Inc. York Beach, ME. 2003

Moser, Mary Beth Honoring Darkness: Exploring the Power of Black Madonnas in Italy Dea Madre Publishing, Vashon Island, WA 2005.

Nezami, Ganjavi & Colin Turner {Trans.} *Layla and Majnun* John Blake Publishing, London U.K. 1997

Neumann, Erich *The Great Mother*
Mythos Books, Princeton University Press; Princeton, NJ 1972.

Oleszkiewicz-Peralba, Malgorzata *The Black Madonna in Latin America and Europe: Tradition and Transformation* University of New Mexico Press NM, 2007.

Patai, Raphael The Hebrew Goddess Wayne State University Press; 3rd edition Detroit, MI. 1990

Perera, Sylvia Brinton Descent to the Goddess (Studies in Jungian Psychology) Inner City Books, Toronto, Canada 1981.

Plaskow, Judith Weaving the Visions: New Patterns in Feminist Spirituality HarperCollins San Francisco, CA 1989

Plaskow, Judith The Coming of Lilith: Essays on Feminism, Judaism, and Sexual Ethics, 1972-2003 Beacon Press, Boston, MA. 2005.

Robinson, James M. *The Nag Hammadi Library* HarperCollins San Francisco, CA. 1990.

Schaberg, Jane. *Resurrection of Mary Magdalene: Legends, Apocrypha, and the Christian Testament.* Continuum, Inc. New York, NY U.S.A. 2002

Schearing, Linda S. (Editor), Ziegler, Valarie H. (Editor), Kvam, Kristen E. (Editor) *Eve & Adam: Jewish, Christian, and Muslim Readings on Genesis and Gender* Indiana University Press, Indiana,
U.S.A. 1999

Thurston, Bonnie. *Women in the New Testament* Crossroad Publishing Company. New York, NY © 1988

Waite, Arthur Edward *Pictorial Key to the Tarot* Weiser Books, Newburyport, MA. 1975.

Wallis Budge, E. A. *Legends of the Egyptian Gods: Hieroglyphic Texts and Translations* Dover Publications Minneola, NY 1994 (Reprint).

Warner, Marina *Alone of all her sex: the myth and the cult of the Virgin Mary* Random House, New York. 1976.

Wilshire, Donna *Virgin Mother Crone: Myths and Mysteries of the Triple Goddess Inner Traditions*, Rochester, VT 1993

Crucible Publications LLC

Rite of Lilith
Copyright © 2017 John F. Rychlicki III
All rights reserved.

To order wholesale, please contact:
American Wholesale Book Company (205) 956-4151
Ingram Book Company (800) 937-8000
Baker & Taylor (800) 775-1100

Crucible Publications Phoenix Arizona, 85008 U.S.A.

Crucible Publications is a publishing house for the 21st century, not the 20th.

Crucible Publications produces & invests in neoteric and visionary artists, writers, and musicians bringing an unconventional vision of art and literature. The company began in 2008 to produce the works of renaissance and neoteric oriented creators, leading us into the 21st century.